The

Perot

Potential

The
Perot
Potential

How a Reformed Ross Perot and the American People can Solve Our Country's Problems

Bob Galbraith, Professor
Crafton Hills College
11711 Sand Canyon Road
Yucaipa, California 92399

First Edition

Nation Publishers

The Perot Potential

How a Reformed Ross Perot and the American People can Solve Our Country's Problems

Nation Publishers
10260 Hope Lane
Yucaipa, California 92399

Ordering information: see back of book.

First Printing 1993

Library of Congress Catalog Card Number: 93-87519

ISBN 0-9640084-0-8

7.95
$14.95 Soft Cover

Printed in the United States of America

ACKNOWLEDGEMENTS

Many assisted me as this book was written, some more than others but all vital to the final work. Although they did not agree with many of the proposals presented, they graciously supported an attempt to solve our problems. They include Roland Bergthold, Chris Biffle, Richard Booth, Harriet Blume, T. L. Brink, Sherri Bruner-Jones, Betty Byron, Neil Campbell, Sara and Gordon Clopine, Jay Edwards, Jim Gerdes, Bart Griffith, Ed Guastad, Judy Hert, Jim Holbrook, Jim Hall, Maritza Hamann, Tom Irwin, Gene Kadow, Trudy Kennedy, Nancy Kiesewetter, Steve Lockhard, Farhad Mansourian, Chuck Menley, Gordon Munro, Mario Perez, Claudia Pompan, Virginia and Peter Rogalsky, Roger Schmidt, Walt Schueling, Vickie Sowers, Laurens Thurman, Bob Turley, Susan Vajna, Bob Wiens, and Laura Winningham. The cover was designed by Karen Logan. My apologies to any others who were inadvertently omitted.

I would also like to express my appreciation to the authors listed in the bibliography. I attempted to cite their work accurately and apologize for any errors or omissions. All opinions expressed are my own and do not necessarily represent the views of any contributors or H. Ross Perot and United We Stand America.

Finally two people were critical to the successful completion of this work. My wife Diane, who combined critical analysis with much needed support and infinite patience, and the world's greatest typist, Windy Menley of Computer Words & Design in Banning, California who created order out of chaos.

To the people who can create a better future
for America and the World.

Bob Galbraith

Table of Contents

INTRODUCTION

■ Laurie Myles, a mother of three, picked up her daughter from a Bible study class. She was confronted by two men who demanded her purse. She complied without objection and was then shot in the chest and killed.

■ The national debt is currently in excess of $4.4 trillion and the interest consumes fifteen percent of all government spending.

■ The U.S. border patrol estimates that only one million of the approximately three million illegal immigrants who cross our southern border annually are returned to Mexico.

■ The FBI has warned that the use of nuclear weapons by terrorists within U.S. borders is a potential threat to Americans.

■ Each year one million students leave our schools without graduating.

The Perot Campaign of 1992

Headlines like these, describing our government's continuing inability to solve our major problems, were a prelude to Ross Perot's entrance into the 1992 presidential race. Most political analysts found him interesting but insupportable. As the campaign progressed, detractors amassed a lengthy list of descriptions ranging on the lighter side from an egotistical and opportunistic pitchman to the more critical, a paranoid, egomaniacal dictator. However, a growing numbers of Americans listened to this new candidate and many eventually became supporters. They believed Ross Perot was a potential leader and the only candidate addressing the real problems of America. He was offering workable solutions and demanding the sacrifices necessary to resolve our current dilemma.

Then he surprised the nation by suddenly withdrawing from the race. His supporters were devastated while his opponents, especially the Republicans, were overjoyed. Prior to the election, he made another unprecedented move and reactivated his campaign. Amazingly, this erratic off-again, on-again candidate for the highest office in the land received 19.7 million votes. Nineteen percent of the American voters were frustrated with the failure of the major parties and their candidates, and they cast their ballots for this unpredictable, homespun Texan.[8]

Perot's Options

What will Ross Perot do next? He has several options. He can continue to lead United We Stand America and achieve some minor reforms which are within the political reach of a grassroots, government watchdog group. If, on the other hand, Clintonomics turns sour before the 1996 election, he could propose a marriage of convenience with the Republican party in an attempt to secure their presidential nomination. Perot could probably deliver most of the sixty-two percent of his supporters who were Republican defectors and, along with disillusioned Democrats and hard-core Republicans, possibly win the Presidency.[8] However, victory for Perot and the Republicans would mean business as usual for the country. If Perot signs on as a Republican, he automatically becomes a part of the political establishment. Those who join the team must play by the rules. This would include compromising many of his realistic solutions because they do not serve the powerful special interest groups. The current political game would continue as usual and the Perot presidency would achieve a few beneficial changes as our country continues to deteriorate.

A third choice available to Perot is an attempt to lead our country toward a new and successful future. This would require several major changes in his current strategy. First he must shore up his personal strengths and, most importantly, eliminate his flaws. Then

UWSA should become a political party and convene a national conference. Innovative and talented people from all political backgrounds would be invited to participate. Academic and technical experts, government officials, business and labor leaders and grassroots activists would be directed to place national needs before special interests and collectively develop workable solutions to our country's major problems. These proposals would become the UWSA party platform. Ross Perot would then be declared the presidential candidate. Talented people from around the nation who support the platform could run for Congress. A majority of the American voters would unite behind these believable candidates and Perot and most of the UWSA congressional candidates would win the election. Then the platform could be implemented.

Perot, Reform and Results

The first chapter describes Perot's strong points and then suggests how he can eliminate his faults and lead America into the future. Subsequent chapters present the ideas of various experts regarding both our country's major problems and the solutions to these issues. They include the following proposals:

1. A strong economy as a result of a major reduction in the national debt.
2. Increased personal savings and investments motivated by financial incentives.
3. Greater productivity in business and industry through computers, robotics and cooperative employee groups. Assisted by management at the job site, these groups will refine new ideas and eliminate unnecessary procedures.
4. Increased employment as a skilled work force is developed through education and retraining.
5. Smaller government with incentives for efficiency and productivity. Government will monitor and regulate private sector production of goods and provision of services.
6. Reduced expenditures for excessive and insupportable entitlement programs.
7. New strategies designed to either support or repair American families.

8. Schools which produce students with a better understanding of our world and also the work skills needed in our modern technological society.

9. A reformed health care system, supported primarily by greater efficiency and user taxes on harmful products and activities.

10. A major reduction in the use of illegal drugs and a reformation of our criminal justice system.

11. Environmental preservation with a sustainable earth policy which regulates human population growth, resource consumption and pollution.

12. A return to national energy independence.

13. The reestablishment of family farms using environmentally sustainable agriculture.

14. A modern, efficient and less expensive national defense system which will protect America from external aggression.

15. A strong United Nations international peace-making and peace-keeping program designed to prevent most wars.

16. Foreign aid crafted to support small business and agricultural development in the poor countries of the world—enabling citizens to remain in their country, rebuild their political and economic systems and provide themselves with a prosperous life.

We will be motivated to make these changes by a fear of the loss of our quality of life, and the programs will be maintained with social and economic incentives. They will be undergirded by individual creativity and sacrifice, a revival of our moral, ethical and religious traditions and a renewal of the spirit of America.

Purpose of This Book

This is not an academic treatise written for the intellectual community. The treatment is not complete or exhaustive, and some areas lack specific references or examples. It is a proposal written to the American people, with the hope that they can create a better future for themselves, their children and the world.

CHAPTER ONE

H. ROSS PEROT—THE GOOD, THE BAD AND THE FUTURE

Perot's Strengths

Ross Perot has a variety of qualities which attract supporters. He is a populist and historically the American middle class has been drawn to charismatic leaders with basic, understandable solutions to their problems. Perot effectively uses clever quips, cutting humor and a down-home style which includes "getting under the hood" and "cleaning out the barn". He addresses the major concerns of the American people: the federal debt, crime, jobs and the economic future of our children. Perot is also an educator, and believes that people can comprehend complex problems if they are clearly presented. While his critics scoffed at his nontraditional infomercials on economics, complete with charts and a pointer, millions of Americans watched intently and learned how our $4.4 trillion debt places our nation at economic risk.

As an outsider he strikes hard at the political elite, those government officials who have separated themselves from the people and amassed personal fortunes at taxpayer expense. He even places part of the blame on the people. No traditional politician would say to a group of voters, "If you want to know who is responsible for our problems, look in the mirror". He also tells the American public they can secure the necessary power and make significant changes by becoming actively involved in a new political movement. Hearing these proposals, perhaps for the first time, an increasing number of Americans are willing to join UWSA and work for reform.

Perot also has the ability to defang volatile social issues such as abortion and race relations with a libertarian approach. Thus he avoids the zealots at both extremes and continues to focus on solutions to our nation threatening problems. Also, while our government is burdened with excessive bureaucracy and inefficiency, Perot projects a business-like management style. Coupling this with a military background, he reflects a can-do image. When necessary he will take a calculated and even daring risk as illustrated by the rescue of his employees held hostage in Iran. In addition, as the world enters the information age, he demonstrates an understanding of the power of the media on talk shows, infomercials and electronic town hall meetings.

Finally, he possesses a strong cultural appeal. Most citizens still believe in the American dream, people succeeding through dedication and hard work. With no previous experience as a political office holder, Perot ran as an underdog. The experts claimed he would generate little support. Yet, as he continued to capture the attention of a frustrated citizenry, this dark horse candidate came from behind, gradually gaining on the favorites and finished with significant support.

These are some of Perot's major strengths. However, he does have significant flaws and as a result, a large majority of the voters did, and still do believe that he is not qualified to be president. The way Perot deals with his insufficiencies will determine his future success or failure.

Perot's Flaws

The American political system demands that candidates be carefully scrutinized by the press and Perot did not handle this well. While he enjoyed responding to general questions, his reaction to those which were pointed or personal was mixed. He often avoided the answer, failed to bring his notes on the topic or attempted to rephrase the question. Occasionally he even became hostile or abrasive. In response, the press gleefully searched every nook and cranny of Perot's background and also meticulously dissected each statement and proposal. As a future candidate, he must run the media's gauntlet with his popular positive style. He must also present carefully constructed and detailed proposals.[41]

Some accuse Perot of paranoia. In the 1970s he apparently claimed that the North Vietnamese and Black Panthers planned to kill him.[41] Also, during his recent presidential campaign, he accused the Republicans of hatching a plot to embarrass his family prior to his daughter's wedding.[90] Periodic political assassinations and frequent dirty tricks by opponents tend to support these claims by any candidate. However to avoid criticism in the future, he should increase his personal security and refrain from further comment on these issues.

Some charge that Perot is a former participant in the system of political payoffs he now attacks. Financial contributions to Richard Nixon and Wilbur Mills are said to have lubricated the wheels of government and resulted in the awarding of federal contracts to his company, Electronics Data System.[90] If this is true he should admit the activities and repudiate the practice.

Another criticism is his authoritarian and secretive style of administration. He is accused of directing a small group of like-minded insiders which made the major decisions during his presidential campaign and continue to direct UWSA policy. A number of defecting volunteers contend their ideas and suggestions received little consideration.[90] The direction of political campaigns by a few close-mouthed advisors is common however this does not support Perot's populist image. To resolve this situation, some security and efficiency must be sacrificed in exchange for broad participation. The party must bring in new, diverse and talented people with innovative ideas and give them the power to develop solutions to our problems.

Perot's contradictory statements were another voter concern. The most devastating was his surprising withdrawal from, and then reentry into, the presidential campaign after vowing to remain in the race to the end. This was a major blow to his credibility. To prevent a repeat of this type of error, future political strategy and procedures must be skillfully crafted and then faithfully followed.

Perot attempted to address many of our major problems in a brief period of time with limited input. As a result, general solutions proposed with great confidence were later found to be vague, contradictory or lacking in the complexity necessary for successful implementation. For example, some economic experts claim that his plan to eliminate the national debt in only five years would prevent a recovery from the current recession.[90] Again, in the future, detailed programs should be carefully designed by a diverse group of experts.

Can Perot Win?

If UWSA becomes a political party and Ross Perot runs for president, can he and the UWSA congressional candidates win? The answer lies in Perot's present strength, future actions and resulting image. He still retains significant support. Some surveys suggest that his current following may consist of as much as twenty-five percent of the electorate.[18] Others indicate that as a result of his methods used in fighting NAFTA, the number may be much lower. Although he has his faults, none are insurmountable. If he maintains and develops his strong points, corrects his flaws and includes a variety of skilled and dedicated people in the development of a party platform, he and his party's congressional candidates could win the support of a majority of the American voters. Because he is a reformer with no previous political and economic commitments to the special interests, he could implement new, nontraditional and workable solutions.

Finally, at this time, there are no other political outsiders who possess his popularity, financial resources and capacity to solve our problems. If we want a new America, H. Ross Perot and his UWSA is the only game in town. We must also realize that time is on his side. Indications are that our major problems will worsen and cause more disgruntled Americans to look beyond our two major political parties for real solutions.

CHAPTER TWO

AN OVERVIEW—PROBLEMS AND SOLUTIONS

The Optimists

Perot faces a nation which is asking itself a fundamental question. Where is America going? The answer depends upon who is asked. Many well-educated, highly motivated and financially successful Americans are generally optimistic. They are working at a dependable, high-paying position and many own their own home. Their busy lives are filled with the daily obligations of job, family and recreation. Although our country does have problems, they believe that our society is basically stable and our future is secure. They would argue that although America has had its ups and downs, conditions have generally improved and today we are the strongest economic and military power in the world. In response to our current financial downturn, business and industry are adopting new technology and eliminating unnecessary expenditures. As a result, our economy will begin to grow again, employment will increase and our tax base will expand. Government will then have the necessary funds to meet our country's social needs including crime prevention, education and environmental improvement and also gradually reduce the national debt. By working harder within our two major political parties and continuing to follow our democratic traditions, we will slowly but surely work out compromises which will solve our problems.

The Pessimists

Others would disagree. Some well-to-do Americans, along with a growing number of middle class and working poor, believe they are losing access to the American dream. Although they cannot identify a clear, single threat, just below the thin veneer of normalcy they perceive deep cracks in our nation's basic foundation. This view is supported by televised images which bring a daily dose of, for the most part, bad news from the nation and around the world. The newscast moves quickly from one depressing item to the next, describing increasing violence, disorder, deceit and greed. The problems are never solved, they are only repeated at another time and place. These Americans feel that our country is adrift. We seem to have no positive, long-term national game plan for success and simply react in a knee-jerk manner to a series of newsworthy problems and calamities.

People's Responses

Individuals respond to this perceived situation in different ways. Out of frustration, many reach for a quick fix. Longer prison sentences are proposed to solve the growing problem of crime. However without addressing the many causes, they see more criminals quickly rotate through our overcrowded and expensive prisons and crime increasing in their communities. Others become cynical and in response to their slow, continuous losses, they develop an island mentality and attempt to retreat to the apparent safety of home, family and friends. Some sell out and attempt to escape by moving to another area, only to find that the problems have followed them. Many turn against others, trying to secure what they believe is their rightful piece of a shrinking American pie. From corporate board rooms to crime ridden urban slums, they struggle for a larger share of our diminishing resources. In doing so, they resemble those proverbial passengers who, as the Titanic sailed from port, argued over the best deck chairs.

The Good News

But there is a flip side to this depressing assessment. A careful search reveals thousands of brave and ingenious people who believe that failure should be overcome, not tolerated. Individually or in groups they have developed unique and successful solutions to enormous problems. These creative, adventurous people defy the traditional, respected and powerful establishment and proclaim that many of the current familiar and comfortable methods must be changed. They range from highly-educated individuals using sophisticated technology to average citizens employing trial and error methods. These people are found everywhere; in business and industry, grassroots groups or individually tinkering at home with a new idea. Some remain within business or government, attempting to subvert failed bureaucracies with new and workable techniques. Others leave faltering organizations and move out into a perilous world in search of creative freedom. These exciting people have shown that there are solutions to our problems.

Why Problems Are Not Solved

If this is true, why haven't the existing solutions been implemented? Unfortunately, they are stalled for at least two reasons. First, both of our major political parties are controlled by special interest groups. Using campaign contributions, they direct the politicians to serve their needs and wants. This results in the passage of specific, beneficial legislation and the selective enforcement of laws by regulatory agencies. These special-interest groups are not inherently evil. Many Americans hold membership in one or more of these organizations. However, their increasing power over the political process results in group benefits at the expense of our national interest. Second, the public is, for the most part, misinformed by our commercial media. Television, directed by viewer ratings and sponsors profits, often presents visually exciting symptoms rather than basic problems and their solutions. Dan Rather recently denounced his profession for replacing foreign reports and in-depth news analysis with mayhem, gossip and fluff.

The lack of both political control over their own lives and clear and accurate information regarding our major problems, has produced a divided citizenry. As our situation worsens, special-interest groups seek more power and create greater divisions. Because of their massive political and economic debts to these groups, and their overwhelming desire to be reelected, the politicians in the Democratic and Republic parties no longer represent the best interests of our nation.

Possible Solutions—Grassroots Groups

United We Stand America is a large and powerful grassroots group. Can it reform our political system? Most professional politicians admit that a primary source of political power and an avenue for renewal in a democracy is the grassroots citizen movements. These include groups organized to fight crime (Neighborhood Watch), drunk driving (Mothers Against Drunk Driving) and environmental destruction (Audubon Society). Most grassroots political groups have a similar strategy. First, a small group of dedicated activists organize in an attempt to solve a problem which they believe the government is not adequately addressing. They meet together, become informed about the issues and then promote their cause in a variety of ways. Some write letters to politicians or attend government meetings and testify. Others picket and a few even break the law by blocking access to buildings or sabotaging equipment and facilities. Their activities prick the conscience of a larger, sympathetic group which will supply moral and financial support and in some cases, eventually become activists themselves. The real power of these citizen groups is in their personal dedication to the goal. No amount of money can purchase this willingness to work endlessly for reform.

If their cause is just in the eyes of a large number of people, the movement will gradually grow and some of the demanded changes will eventually be incorporated into law by the political process. If the cause is ignored or actively opposed by most people, the group will either continue to function with a small number of supporters or disappear. Although many important changes have gradually occurred in democratic societies as a result of the efforts of citizen activists, there are problems which often prevent major reforms. Activists and their proposed changes can be suppressed for long periods of time by government officials who stand behind the rule of law, even if some of the laws are unjust. These officials have the political and economic superiority necessary to maintain their power. Grassroots movements will continue to prod the government into needed reforms as citizen activists slowly accumulate political and financial support for their cause. Unfortunately, because our country's enormous problems can only be solved through major changes, we cannot depend entirely upon the slow gathering of consensus and the eventual implementation of reforms initiated by these groups.

Single Party Control

Let's look at another possible solution. Some politicians suggest that our problems will be solved if, as in our current administration, one of our major political parties wins both the presidency and a congressional majority. They claim that this will provide the unanimity needed to enact reform legislation. Given this possibility, which of the two major political parties should be chosen to assume the leadership of the government and solve our basic national problems? Neither, since both control and benefit from the current unworkable system. The Democrats and the Republicans carry historical and traditional baggage which prevents them from meeting our national needs. Their overwhelming determination to be reelected and the resulting enslavement to campaign contributors along with their acquiescence to conflicting groups of voters, prevents any meaningful reform. Their response to the need for change has been to retreat into their monolithic, marble bunkers and wallow in the morass of self-created, non-productive procedures. No reformational dynamite will succeed in blasting them out of their political fortress.

A New Political Party

Since neither major political party can solve America's central problems, we must turn to another solution: one which is both familiar and unsuccessful, the formation of a new party. This proposal appears to be politically insupportable. Historically, third parties in the United States have emerged as a result of dissent among a significant number of citizens. They raise important issues, initiate debate and, as a result, educate the public.[178] However, few candidates have been elected to office because these new parties are usually built around a single issue or reflect only the narrow philosophy of their presidential candidate. Libertarians focus on removing government from most areas of American life and establishing the complete privatization of society. George Wallace's American Independent Party is traditional, segregationist and generally opposed to the power of the federal government over states' rights.

Third parties also have difficulty building a national organization. Finally, any valid planks in their political platform are usually absorbed by one of the two primary parties. Robbed of their important issues and left with only minor reforms, they either continue to function at an insignificant level or recede into oblivion.

Why a Third Party?

If the history of third parties in America is one of failure, why propose a new party to solve our country's most pressing concerns? We are in a unique period of American history. Changes are occurring at blinding speed. We are faced with new employment needs, changing family structure, rising crime, increased pollution, massive immigration and a new and different role in world politics. While our two major parties are mired in a traditional system of political and economic debt to the special interests, a United We Stand Party led by Ross Perot would be free of these obligations and could effectively come to grips with our major problems and simultaneously develop new, realistic and workable solutions.

Function of the New Party

In order to meet our national needs, the party platform must be developed by America's most talented people. This can be accomplished in a national conference which deals with crime, economic development, education and all of our other major national issues. Those attending will include grassroots workers who have been grappling with the problem for years and, in the process, have created small, successful solutions. They can unite with university scholars who have formulated theories from a careful study of the overall problem. Joining them, technical experts will maximize the efficiency of the proposed solutions by bringing computer analysis, teleconferencing and other appropriate technology to the table. Finally progressive leaders from business, industry and labor will represent American capitalism.

Currently working models can be analyzed, and if successful, improved with modern technology. Also new solutions will be proposed, studied and, if sound, prepared for implementation. Delegates will search for win-win solutions, those in which all parties benefit most and sacrifice least. All proposals will be measured by their potential to improve the nation rather than one group at the expense of another. The negative impact of necessary changes will be softened with job transfer or retraining. Workable ideas from the conference will be integrated into a long-term plan of national action which, when implemented, will be continuously monitored and modified to insure success. This will become the platform of the United We Stand America party.

The Role of Business and Industry

The support of the forward-looking leaders of business and industry is critical to the success of this new political party. Why would those who currently exert extensive control over our political process relinquish what is for them a winning system? While many individual companies continue to grow and prosper, some business leaders realize that a productive and profitable corporate climate cannot be maintained in the midst of a declining society. They see a failing educational system generating fewer skilled workers while crime, drug use and poor worker health reduce productivity. The lack of functional families and communities create a greater dependency on government and a growing demand for social services which draws money and resources away from other citizen and national needs. They know that these problems are compounded by the enormous waste of financial, natural and energy resources through both government and corporate inefficiency and corruption. They also realize that our enormous national debt is causing other industrialized nations to question our economic integrity and ability to remain a world leader. Thus it is proposed that the major leaders of business and industry, whose goal is the maximization of profits, will participate in a new political party because it is in their own best economic interest to do so. The thread of concern for our future can weave together the best interests of both sustainable business and the nation and give rise to a new America.

Who Will Pay?

Grand ideas but as always we must move to the bottom line and ask the key question: Who will pay for these new programs? Apparently the money is already available. A reoccurring theme which pervades this book is the enormous amount of money which is wasted at all levels in both government and business. Future chapters describe the annual waste of $400 billion in government[81] and $1.7 trillion in our total economy.[22] We criticize this waste but at the same time, from individual workers to the highest level of management, we carefully guard our individually accumulated perks. A national commitment to reduce waste, inefficiency, greed and corruption at all levels of every organization could generate an enormous amount of "free money" to support needed programs.

Why Support Perot and UWSA?

Without a "track record" of success, what will cause a majority of the American voters to support a reformed Ross Perot and the United We Stand America party? Why will the people of this country cooperate, compromise and even sacrifice hard won individual gains for the "benefit of the nation"? Their motivation will be a shared and driving fear of the loss of our quality of life. Through accurate, quality educational programs developed by the UWSA conferences and dispersed through the media, people will understand the subtle, harmful effects of our current national problems on both their individual lives and the future of their children. This information will also demonstrate how access to a safe, prosperous and enjoyable life for our citizens can be achieved through carefully designed solutions.

Despite public education, many may not accept the idea of a new political party. They may not perceive our current situation as an immediate threat to their personal well being and be unwilling to make the changes and sacrifices necessary to implement proposed solutions. However these citizens may be moved to change in the future by either the fear of, or an actual disaster. We have experienced two events in our recent history which have resulted in major voluntary changes in attitude and behavior. One is World War II. After the attack on Pearl Harbor, most Americans supported a congressional declaration of war. The result was an immediate unification of the people and a total, long-term commitment of all necessary resources. Citizens changed their lifestyles and sacrificed individual and group needs and wants to support the war effort. As a result, victory was achieved. Another example is the depression of the

1930's. In the economic chaos, many people lost their savings, their jobs and in some cases their homes. Today only elderly Americans remember the years of deprivation: life with only the barest essentials and in some cases the hours waiting in bread lines. But America pulled together under strong national leadership and after many years of effort and a world war, experienced an economic recovery.

Is there a possibility that our current political path could lead to a war or an economic depression? With the collapse of world communism, most experts discount the possibility of a future world war. However, we are currently involved in two types of warfare which could quickly expand with devastating consequences. The first is international terrorism. The attack on the World Trade Center in New York has been dismissed by most because there were only a few deaths and minor injuries. However, if chemical, biological or nuclear weapons, which are available on the world market, had been used, the death and destruction would have been enormous and unprecedented in American history. America is also participating in an increasing number of military engagements in politically unstable, developing countries. Some of these nations have, or will soon possess, weapons of mass destruction. As we attempt to maintain national and world stability and protect our access to both Middle Eastern petroleum and other necessary imports, future foreign military conflicts could erupt into chemical, biological or nuclear wars. The results would be injury and death to thousands of American troops and the possible contamination of our country via high altitude winds. The outcome of "Desert Storm" could have been much different if the invasion of Kuwait had occurred at a later date when Iraq had functional nuclear weapons.

Is there another economic depression in our future? A few economists make a case for future financial collapse however most suggest that the size of our economy and the numerous checks and balances will prevent this type of disaster. However, most economists are concerned about the financial impact of the national debt which is addressed in Chapter Four. Its size is difficult to comprehend—in excess of $4 trillion. The interest payments now consume fifteen percent of all government spending. This amount is equal to the combined current government expenditures for health, science, space, agriculture, housing, environmental protection and admini-

stration of justice. Current solutions proposed by the two major parties do not even attempt to reduce the debt, only its rate of growth.[105]

The possibility, or actual occurrence, of a continuing decline in
our social systems, devastating terrorist attacks against Americans on
our own soil, increasing military engagements in developing countries and a growing, massive and unsustainable debt could tip the
scales in favor of Perot and the United We Stand America party. With
carefully studied solutions, they could capture the imagination of the
American people, galvanize public opinion and win the election.

CHAPTER THREE

POLITICS AND GOVERNMENT

Introduction

The American political system, the prototype for those who seek freedom and democracy, is no longer able to solve the major problems of this country. Our government now functions primarily to benefit the leaders and some of the members of wealthy and politically active organizations including business, industry, labor, agriculture and retired persons. These power brokers gather money from organizational profits and individual members and distribute these funds through their PACs (political action committees) or by direct contributions primarily to the incumbent politicians of both parties to support their reelection campaigns. After the election, a hoard of lobbyists descend upon the victorious politicians and assist them in designing laws and government programs which will benefit their financial supporters. Thus the process of majority rule is disrupted.

The American public must also share some of the blame for our current situation. We have been duped by politicians into believing that the government can meet all of our individual wants and at the same time solve the complex problems of our society. This is what we want to hear, however it is not true. The demands of individuals and small groups are often in opposition to and thus block solutions to our national problems.

Middle Class

This entire floundering political and economic system is financed primarily by the middle class. While they are paying the bills they are earning decreasing real wages, paying a larger percentage of their income in taxes and receiving few government benefits. Many attempt to adapt by working longer and harder; however they are gradually losing access to the American dream as their economic security, social structures and environment collapse around them. Families, in their various forms, are racked by increasing unemployment, poverty, abuse of women and children, divorce, substance abuse and violent crime. American education deteriorates in overcrowded and under-funded schools. The physical and mental health of many Americans declines because they do not have access to adequate health care. Our air and water are polluted and our ecosystems continue to fall victim to sprawling urbanization and the excessive harvest of our natural resources. Modern agribusiness destroys our topsoil and degrades our aquifers with excessive chemical fertilizers and pesticides.

World Problems

Our political problems extend beyond our shores. The poor, developing countries are threatened by a human population explosion, grinding poverty, and continuing wars between traditional enemies. If these conditions persist, insurrection and anarchy will increase in countries which are vital to our national interest inevitably drawing us into more "Desert Storm-like" military conflicts. The continuing chaos in these countries will increase international terrorism and also unleash a massive migration of refugees into America, Europe and the developed countries of Asia.

A Divided Nation

Without significant political power or visionary national leadership to provide long-term social, moral, political and economic goals, many Americans have turned against each other in an attempt to meet their short-term needs and wants. We are a nation divided into a variety of opposing groups based upon wealth, race, and position on specific issues. The daily newspaper identifies the long list of combatants: the wealthy protecting their position against the middle class and the poor, whites and minorities opposing each other, labor versus management, pro-life screaming at pro-choice, liberals attempting to block the proposals of conservatives, and as always,

Republicans against Democrats. The concern is not that these groups disagree. The diverse mixture of people with both divergent viewpoints and personal freedom has been the historic crucible from which the exciting and ingenious ideas of Americans have been forged. But in this complex and confusing time, we have become narrowly focused and are now placing our individual and group interests above those of our nation. Many Americans who could be a part of the rebuilding of our country see no valid solutions proposed and have opted out of our political system. Less than half of those who are eligible to vote have registered, and in many elections, fewer than fifty percent of the registered voters participate.

Response of Politicians

The response of our lifetime politicians to these major national problems is to arm themselves with campaign contributions and carefully attend to their primary goal— becoming reelected. And most of them succeed. In the 1988 national elections, ninety-eight percent of the incumbent candidates were returned to the House of Representatives and in the Senate, an almost equally overwhelming eighty-five percent were reelected.[37] This phenomenal return resembles the predictable migration of a flock of birds which comes back to the same secure and productive feeding area year after year.

The reelection of incumbents in the legislative and the executive branches of our government begins with modern polling techniques which determine the needs and desires of the various groups of voters. Then the political tightrope walk begins. Standing high in the air and away from the real problems of the people, the skillful politician traverses the small rope through the circus we call an election. A political balance is maintained by quickly bending and leaning in different directions toward each of the various politically powerful groups as well as the voting public. A successful campaign also requires extensive television advertising. Usually the candidate with the largest war chest is able to purchase the most expensive television marketing program and win the election. Senators running for re-election in 1990 were raising an average of $145,000 per day to support their bid for reelection.[37]

After the carefully orchestrated political campaign is concluded, most Americans find no forward-looking leaders with solutions to our real problems and they seldom support candidates with a fervent zeal. Many yearn for even one brave candidate who will tell Americans the truth—that in order to solve our national problems, we must first make major changes in our political system. But progressive politicians cannot propose these changes without offending large, powerful wealthy groups and, as a result, losing the next election.

Some desperate voters attempt to change our government by turning out all of the incumbents and hoping that new office holders will reform the system. But even if newly elected officials are sincere, they will be unsuccessful. The rules of the game remain the same. In order to become reelected, all politicians must participate in the corrupt system.

The charade goes on and in the end the middle class is relegated to a dismal search for a few beneficial scraps among the complex proposals of a distant and failing government.

After the Election

After winning the election, members of Congress must produce a variety of showcase legislation in an attempt to meet the conflicting demands of the various PACs, individual donors and voting groups. In order to succeed, they must gain the support of other congress persons who are trying to do the same thing for the voters in their district. And so they embrace one another in a dance of mutual political courtship. This "pork barrel polka" continues indefinitely as politicians negotiate with each other to bring enormously expensive and often unneeded government benefits to those with an inordinate amount of political influence. In the end, the few voters who are rewarded are bribed with some of their own money: a government contract, a farm subsidy or some other benefit in return for their federal taxes or PAC contributions.

Delegation of Power

As politicians attempt to meet the many demands of their financial benefactors, their colleagues and their constituents, they often find that they cannot remain fully informed regarding the variety of technically complex issues surrounding proposed legislation. In response, they delegate their power to those who are not accountable to the voters. This includes their political staff, the lobbyists who represent the special interest groups or the governmental agency bureaucrats whose primary concern is to maintain their position and insure that their agency will continue to grow and prosper. Politicians are often reduced to television performers delivering glowing speeches crafted by skilled script writers with near academy award winning quality. The voters fall into the entertainment trap by rating them on the quality of their performance rather than their accomplishments.

Political Decisions

As the time for a required decision draws near, politicians become fearful of offending one or more of the special interest groups or the voting public. Since most of our problems have no simple or inexpensive solutions, our representatives are often gripped with partial or complete paralysis as they watch them grow and worsen. Rather than interpreting change and leading the American people into the future, they wait and hope for the formation of a national consensus. But because our society is so sharply divided, this unity does not occur. When politicians are finally forced to make a decision, it is usually too late to provide a successful solution.

Government Agencies

Not only are politicians failing to lead America, but the governmental agencies which were established to implement legislation do not function effectively. Their carefully constructed organizational charts with detailed chains of command result in uniform, inflexible, top-down control of all activities. They are designed to follow policies and procedures rather than to quickly and efficiently produce results. The lumbering giants continue to grind out numerous memos and reports while accomplishing little. Their functions often overlap and many activities are duplicated because the problems of the real world do not fall into the neatly arranged boxes of the organizational framework.[142] Administrators lack the skills or courage necessary to run the agency effectively. They often protect turf, resist change and attempt to build empires. In order to maintain their position, these politically appointed directors limit agency activities to those which are favorable to the current administration.

Government Employees

Meanwhile, agency employees are forced into the organizational mold of conformity. They must adhere to a detailed job description, follow rules and regulations and document their activities with numerous memos. Their administrative evaluation is based upon how well they follow the procedures rather than how successfully they serve the public. This fallacious definition of successful work, together with strong unions, provides an employee with a job for life at a dependable income regardless of their productivity. Since innovation and extra work by new, young or talented employees is frowned upon by other workers and unrewarded by government, these potential sources of renewal either conform and become expert paper shufflers or, because they are frustrated with a failing process, leave government employment.[142]

Government Efficiency

When people demand more service from their government, agencies respond not by increasing efficiency but by growing in size and increasing expenses and fees. If the public refuses to support an increase in cost, politicians make selective cuts in those agencies which are deemed less important by the politically powerful. But this does not improve efficiency because government waste is not concentrated in small extractable pockets; it is an integral part of the system, is imbedded in every agency and permeates the entire structure like a malignant cancer.

Reform of Political Campaign Financing.

In order to solve our major problems we must change both our political processes and governmental functions. The first major change will be the way we pay for political campaigns. Attempts to reform the process usually fall into one of three categories. First a limit on the size of a donation from each individual or group. However many organizations can remain within current or proposed limits and still secure desired favors from politicians. When more contributions are needed to influence politicians, a "steering committee" is formed and the group pools contributions with others who have similar interests. This enables them to achieve their mutual goals. The second is a limit on the total amount a candidate may accept. If this proposal is implemented, the results will probably be a rush to donate, those arriving first purchasing the greatest amount of influence. Those remaining will search for loopholes or simply spend their money "independently" to support a candidate. A third proposal is the establishment of equal campaign spending limits for each candidate in a race. However this provides a built-in advantage for the incumbent with name and news recognition, free postage and hired staff, all of which can be used to support a reelection bid. Although these proposals have merit, we must realize that some of the best minds in our country are dedicated to finding a way around or through any regulations which limit or prevent them from manipulating the political process to their advantage.

There seems to be only one procedure which can break the strangle hold of the wealthy and powerful on our political system, public financing of election campaigns. The last thing most Americans want is another political hand in their pocket; this time fishing out money to pay for television time and posters. But if this proposal eliminates the privileges of special interest groups, taxpayers can actually save money. Lets look at an example. If in the next election, public funds provide the same total amount which was spent on elections for the House of Representatives in 1988, each candidate will receive $250,000. But this merely shifts the source of money from the private to the public sector. Where is the savings for taxpayers in the proposal? We can attempt to answer this with an illustration. As a result of their power over the political process, from 1955 to 1989 the percentage of total federal taxes paid by corporations dropped from 27.3 percent to 11.0 percent. The slack was picked up by individual taxpayers or added to the national debt. If the corporate tax contribution had not been reduced over this period of time, in one year, 1989, they would have paid an additional $159 billion. This amount could provide public financing for both House and Senate general elections for more than 300 years.[39]

If we move to public support of political campaigns, funds can be allocated as follows; candidates nominated by the two major parties will receive a fixed amount of public funds only if they agree to use no other financial sources. Some candidates may choose not to accept limited public funds and turn to wealthy contributors. But if they raised more than their opponent, public funds will increase to

match the private donations. Since no donor advantage can be
gained by making private contributions, these private financial gifts
will probably decline and perhaps end.[39]

If implemented, this proposal can also be constantly monitored
to prevent "loophole lizards" by requiring candidates to report all
supportive, independent expenditures, donations to both candidates
and parties, speaking fees and gifts. They would also sign binding
agreements to prevent after-office awards of lucrative jobs or payments. Violators will be reported to the Federal Election Commission and unlike current practice, be vigorously punished or
disqualified.

This proposal assumes that one or both of the major political
parties will reform the election process. However since this will not
happen, how can a third party win under these conditions? Clawson
proposes that if third parties receive a minimum of five percent of the
vote they will be retroactively funded, as was John Anderson in 1980,
and also be eligible for funding in future elections.

Informed Voters

Turning to other types of election reform, we must also increase
voter access to accurate, unbiased political information. Information
banks regarding the candidates and the issues can be developed by
the League of Women Voters and other politically neutral groups. In
exchange for tax write-offs, commercial television will make this information available along with candidate debates and thus reduce the
cost of the publicly-funded campaigns. While making political campaigns fair, we must also make government work for all of the people.

A New Role for Government.

Most would agree that government is too large, inefficient and
often corrupt. Political reform must change many of the functions of
government. Some government activities will increase. This includes directing, coordinating, monitoring, maintaining quality control and setting priorities. Most areas will be greatly reduced. Goods
and services can be provided to the public by designing contracts
with specific performance criteria, accepting competitive bids and
provide funding based upon successful performance. Current gov-

ernment provided services such as welfare, education and fire and police protection can be carried out more efficiently, effectively and inexpensively by carefully monitored private enterprise, nonprofit agencies or volunteer groups. As this transformation gradually occurs, most government employees will successfully move into the private sector supported by retraining and their previous background and experience in the field. Using their creative talents and ingenuity, they will successfully secure private employment or government contracts for public services, provide greater customer satisfaction, develop pride in their work and higher personal income.

In order to gain the confidence of and truly represent all Americans, the government will also provide people with access to both political power and private ownership. When government is decentralized and people are empowered to make decisions at the bottom or around the edges of a society, there is greater citizen commitment and less waste. Political power must also be accompanied by access to private ownership. Through economic incentives, lending institutions can be encouraged to loan to more individuals. People care for and protect what they own. Those who own their homes or businesses, or experience business ownership through profit sharing will, in an attempt to protect their investment, join with others to maintain the surrounding community. They often voluntarily assume government functions and quickly solve their own problems in an efficient manner. One example is community security. With the assistance of the police, owners who are on site and have a financial investment in the community often effectively enforce rules of proper behavior. Thus security increases while the cost of law enforcement declines. Other examples of the value of private ownership include the maintenance of owner occupied versus public housing, the success of small entrepreneurial businesses, and volunteer groups in communities for crime prevention, recycling and teacher assistance[142]

Governmental agencies will also shift from rule-driven bureaucracies to mission-oriented agencies. The mission is a specific government activity such as directing the building of a bridge. Once the mission has been clearly identified, the only rules and procedures used are those which enable the project to be accomplished (within the other needs and regulations of society). Mission-driven programs include innovation, flexibility and create high morale among workers. Budgets can be designed around the mission rather than governmental departments or agencies. They are small, carefully monitored, and the only purchases are those necessary to complete the task. Flexibility, allows money to be moved quickly to different categories and the project to be completed more efficiently.

The mission also determines the staff. Employees with the needed skills are brought together from different governmental agencies. Once they are assembled, individual initiative and creativity is encouraged. Employees are not penalized for trying new ideas even if they are sometimes unsuccessful. Group cooperation is encouraged with a no-layoff policy and extensive recognition of success. Finally, when the project has been successfully completed, the exact financial and personnel costs can be determined.[142]

Conclusion

In a democracy, government should be a group of people who are hired by the citizens to carry out those activities which best serve the community, state and nation. When the American people understand how our current political system malfunctions and are provided with realistic and workable alternatives, they will support the necessary reforms. The vehicle for these reforms will be Ross Perot and the UWSA political party.

CHAPTER FOUR

ECONOMICS, BUSINESS AND EMPLOYMENT

Economic Groups

Based upon their economic well-being, Americans have become at least three different and often separate groups of people. The first, the rich, are getting richer. Between 1980 and 1987 the wealthiest five percent of the American people experienced an increase in income of seventeen percent. Currently forty-five percent of the U.S. income is gathered by the richest twenty percent of the population.[74] The wealthy are able to continuously improve their own quality of life by taking advantage of tax loopholes which politicians have created in exchange for campaign contributions. Almost half of our national income is expended for their benefit. Their accumulated wealth is added to the financial resources of the global elite and invested in economically profitable stocks, bonds or property. Those who are experiencing the American dream are primarily the well-to-do minority.

A majority of Americans are members of the second group, the industrious, hard-working middle class. Previously, these citizens also experienced an improving quality of life. But this is no longer true. In recent years the income of a majority of the young, middle class American families has either remained the same or declined. As a group they are earning $1,500 less in real dollars than young families earned in 1979.[183] Excluding agriculture, the earnings for production workers in America decreased from $319 per week in

1980 to $312 per week in 1987.[74] To make matters worse, a large percentage of their income is taken by the Internal Revenue Service and in the future their taxes will continue to increase in order to pay for promised government entitlements and the growing interest on the national debt. While assuming most of the national tax burden, the middle class receives comparatively few benefits. The government returns only half of its available income to assist the majority of the American people.[154] Caught in the downward economic whirlpool of lower real wages, higher taxes and reduced government benefits, men, women and often children attempt to maintain or improve their quality of life by working long hours: many at two or more jobs. Yet despite their efforts, they are only running faster on an accelerating financial treadmill.

The third group, the working poor, have few resources and many have little hope. Increased immigration and fewer jobs for unskilled workers have resulted in higher unemployment and a major decline in their quality of life. Many have no opportunity to break into the middle class and are becoming an increasing social and financial burden on our society.

History—Presidents Johnson and Carter

Our current economic problems have historical origins. In 1964, in order to pay for the war in Vietnam and the Great Society's social programs, President Johnson ordered the printing of the needed dollars and inflation quickly followed. Then, during the Carter administration, inflation reached eighteen percent. Congress added to the damage by applying COLAs (automatic cost of living adjustments) to federal pensions, social security benefits and Medi-Care. This automatically increased benefits and government spending regardless of government income. Recipients were delighted and, because the raises were quietly automatic, Congress was not constantly accused of increasing spending. The seeds of an unmanageable debt had been planted.

Ronald Reagan

As we entered the 1980's, Ronald Reagan originally envisioned a deregulated, free market economy producing steady growth with low unemployment and inflation. The country would go into debt to stimulate the economy. The increased tax receipts from rising employment and low inflation would allow us to repay this debt at a later date. We could relate to this concept because most Americans had "plastic" and substantial personal debt which we planned to pay off with the higher income generated by our future prosperity. Our economy was bolstered by the entry of foreign money. Japan and the Western European countries were eager to either invest in or purchase outright a part of America and join in the apparently unending economic prosperity. Then there was a tax cut which is always popular with everyone. Reagan also reduced the rate of growth in spending for many social programs. However, there was a subtle downside to his economic policies. He initiated large increases in social security and Medicare benefits while beginning a major defense buildup. President Reagan also continued to support the overvalued U.S. dollar. This reduced exports as fewer foreigners could afford to buy our expensive products. These events caused the federal debt to undergo a quiet but rapid acceleration.

President Bush

President Bush continued most of Reagan's economic policies. As signs of a faltering economy began to appear, few people were concerned. Although many experts stated that our economy had lost much of its ability to respond favorably to a down turn, the administration continued to forecast an optimistic future. Generous unemployment benefits would blunt the impact of any temporary recession, and sufficient government regulatory powers could prevent another depression. Our confidence was reinforced with the arrest of the major stock market decline in October 1989. President Bush continued to project low budget deficits and a high GDP, overestimate tax revenues and maintained off budget financial categories.

The Savings and Loan Disaster

Then we learned of an enormous financial calamity. Because the personal financial impact will occur primarily in the future, there was and still is a benign response to the largest economic loss in the history of the world, the collapse of one out of three American savings and loan institutions. Estimates of the total government (tax-payer) bail out costs are as high as 500 billion dollars.

Two events led to the S & L disaster. First legislative changes enabled these economically conservative lending institutions to gain access to more speculative markets including real estate and junk bonds. At the same time, Congress did not provide careful supervision of this taxpayer insured money. In the end, the financial loss would have been much smaller if the problem had been addressed earlier. Congress saw the disaster coming but decided to do nothing. They knew that it would be politically unwise to derail the longest and largest peace time economic expansion in our history.

Debt and Decline

By this time excessive debt permeated our society. Savings and loan institutions, major insurance companies, cities, states, the federal government and even individuals had accumulated large debts and were operating in a rising sea of red ink. The growing and now massive debt was increased by the recession which began in the fall of 1990. Economic decline was accelerated by increased unemployment. Cuts in government spending resulted in layoffs in defense and related industries. Consumers concerned about personal job security reduced spending which resulted in further job losses in those businesses which produced consumer goods. Less income earned resulted in less taxes paid and reduced government revenue while the cost of unemployment and welfare benefits increased. The Federal Reserve Board attempted to stimulate the economy by reducing interest rates; however, this had little effect.

Today, because of our enormous debt, our government cannot safely use its two previously dependable methods of bringing the country out of a recession: reducing taxes or increasing spending. Our national debt, in excess of $4 trillion, hangs like an economic millstone around our neck.

Solutions—Good Debt and Bad Debt

How can we significantly reduce our national debt and reestablish a sound economy? First we must have a clear understanding of "good debt" and "bad debt".[89] Perhaps this can best be accomplished with a theoretical analogy. Let's assume we decide to buy a car which is needed to drive to work and earn money to make a living. We incur debt because we are willing to make affordable, future monthly payments in order to use the car immediately. The value of the car we purchase, and thus the amount of debt we assume, is determined by our anticipated future income. The larger our paycheck, the more expensive the affordable car. The size of the debt is not important, only the sufficient and dependable future income necessary to make the payments. Later, if for some reason we are unable to make the required payments, we can avoid losing our new car. We simply refinance by borrowing more money. However, this increases the principal, the total interest and the amount of future payments on the debt. Because the total debt has increased, we must also extend the payments further into the future. If we die before the car is paid off, our debt will be passed to our children as a part of our estate.

With this analogy in mind we can differentiate between good debt and bad debt. Good debt is money borrowed for necessary and beneficial expenditures in amounts which can be repaid in a reasonable period of time while maintaining our current quality of life. In the analogy, this is represented by our purchase of a reasonably priced car. Good debt is necessary in an expanding economy. Business needs debt to fund research and development and also expand and modernize with the purchase of new equipment. This type of debt results in greater productivity, higher profits and wages, an increased GNP and tax revenues for government.

Decline of Good Debt—Problems and Solutions

Unfortunately American business and industry has reduced its use of good debt. In the 1980's an amount equal to only 1.8 percent of American GDP was devoted to civilian research and development, while Germany spent 2.6 percent and Japan 2.8 percent.[31] The resulting decline in American productivity was predictable. It decreased from 2.5 percent per year in 1967 to 0.1 percent in 1981.[112]

The use of good debt by business and industry has declined for several reasons. One is a lack of available funds. Returning to our analogy, the use of good debt to purchase our automobile would not be possible if banks had no money to lend. The absence of funds is caused in part by our enormous federal debt which functions like a

growing financial Godzilla monster: feeding ravenously on money
which would normally be available for investment in business and
industry. The solution is obvious; we must significantly reduce federal debt: the mechanism is soon to be discussed.

Funds needed to support good debt are absent for another reason. Americans are failing to save and invest a significant portion of
their income. Rather than placing expendable money in banks or the
stock market, they purchase foreign-made consumer items and
thereby export their wealth to other countries. Americans save only
two percent of their income after taxes. This is the lowest personal
savings rate in the industrialized world.[125] Tax incentives and disincentives can be used to increase savings and investments. Increasing
taxes on luxury items and second homes and a tax reduction on interest derived from savings and capital gains from investments will
drive money from consumption to investment.

National Debt—Good Debt or Bad Debt?

Now let's turn our attention to our $4.4 trillion national debt and
ask the question, "Is this good or bad debt?" It is hard to believe that
anyone would categorize a debt of such magnitude as good. However, returning to our automobile analogy, recall that the amount of
the purchase price and the debt incurred is of no real concern. As
long as we can make the "easy monthly payments" and maintain our
current quality of life, it is good or manageable debt. The ability of
Americans to make the payments on their national debt is determined
by the "national income" or GDP. Since 1952 debt as a percentage
of GDP has varied from twenty-eight to sixty-three percent and in
1988 it was forty-three percent.[89] Since debt is within an historically
acceptable percentage of GDP, some economists argue that it quali-
fies as good debt. This logic assumes one critical point; as the debt
grows, the national income will also increase at a rate necessary to
support the increasing "easy monthly payments". If GDP increased
at a rate of five percent per year, assuming current spending levels,
we could manage our debt. However, our potential economic growth
appears to be three to four percent annually due to the recession of
1991 and low productivity.[126] This eliminates the preferred method
of paying down debt, "growing out" of it by increasing our national
income (GDP) through economic growth. This would enable us to

comfortably make the higher payments. Again, if we apply our automobile analogy, our anticipated future income was overestimated and is now insufficient to meet the required payments. Thus, we must refinance. However, by doing so, we extend the debt further into the future, and as a result increase the total amount due. This financial obligation has now become bad debt because it is reducing our financial security and quality of life and will have an even greater harmful effect on our children and grandchildren. Rather than inheriting our wealth, they will receive an enormous bill.

This depressing future scenario is based upon an optimistic assumption, that our economy will remain intact indefinitely with this enormous debt, a prediction which may not be true. A City Corp Bank study predicted that at the current rate of increase, by 2004 our publicly held national debt will be an insupportable twelve trillion dollars with an annual interest payment of one trillion dollars.[126]

Solutions—Use the "Free" Money

In order to prevent the ultimate collapse of our economy, our government will need to reverse its previous strategy of dealing with debt. The most efficient way to do this is an often stated but seldom implemented formula: reduce waste and corruption. The amount of "free" money which is already in the system and could be diverted for use in a beneficial manner is staggering. In government it is at least $400 billion annually[81] and in our total economy it amounts to $1.7 trillion per year.[22]

Reduce the Cost of Government

Although of lesser significance in terms of the total amount which could be saved, thrift should begin with our politicians as a first step toward restoring the confidence of the American people in their government. Reductions could occur in many areas. Congress employs 20,000 people; about twenty for each Representative and forty per Senator. Congress requires a total annual operating budget of three billion dollars. Congressional consultants absorb an additional amount somewhere between $4.5 and twenty billion per year with some attorneys earning $1,000 per day. And who could expect government officials to spend long, dull hours of travel on Air Force Two without their $57,000 gold-embossed playing cards.[81]

Internal Debt

There are other, more significant ways to decrease spending
and reduce our national debt. Lets consider internal debt, the eighty-
seven percent of the debt we owe ourselves. How can people owe
themselves money? They cannot. This really means some Americans owe money to other Americans. The government raises "spending money" by collecting taxes, primarily from the middle class, and
by selling bonds and securities to upper income individuals, private
organizations and public institutions such as the social security system. The purchasers will benefit in the future by receiving interest
on their investment. The government will pay this interest with
money derived primarily from future middle class taxpayers. Thus
our government's internal debt transfers money from present and anticipated future middle class taxpayers to those who hold bonds and
securities.

Internal debt can be reduced by decreasing the two major government expenditures supported by this process. The first is unnecessary defense spending. The end of the cold war and the emergence
of the "new world order" will enable America to change its strategy
and military expenditures. Although the "how" and "where" will be
hotly debated and carefully studied, we have already begun the process with plans to reduce nuclear weapons and standing armies. If this
is accompanied by a decrease in inefficiency and fraud along with
increased productivity among defense contractors and also a change
in our methods of international conflict resolution (See Chapter
Eleven), we can maintain a strong national defense for less money.

Entitlements

The largest government expense is transfer programs. Social
Security, Medicare, military and federal pensions, welfare and aid to
dependent children are supported primarily by present and anticipated future taxes paid by middle class working people. The total
amounts to forty-one percent of all federal spending and it has become the fastest growing portion of the federal budget. Today almost
half of all Americans receive some type of transfer payment.[125]
Some is distributed to the poor but most is transferred to the well-off
middle aged and elderly. We spend twenty-seven percent of our fed-

eral budget on older Americans. This is eleven times more benefit dollars per person than we spend on the young.[150]

Social Security

The most expensive entitlement program is Social Security. Originally it was designed to assist the elderly poor, however, over the years, politicians have increased and broadened the benefits to this grateful and politically powerful group of citizens. Combined with a dramatic increase in the value of housing through inflation, many aging Americans have become comparatively well to do. Currently older Americans who do not work make more money than younger citizens who do work. In 1985 individuals over 65 years of age received $335 per year more than the average worker. Since Social Security payments are not based upon need, ten percent of these benefits go to households with an income of at least $30,000.[35] Also these benefits are paid to recipients without consideration of the amount they paid into the system. The average person collects all of the money they paid into Social Security in only 2.5 years and then continues to receive an income for another 11.5 years.[125] In order to adequately support the current Social Security and federal retirement systems, the government should have collected an additional 150 billion dollars per year each year for the last fifteen years. Because this did not occur, Social Security and our other federal entitlement programs have a ten trillion dollar unfunded liability. As more people retire and enjoy a longer life, the expense of the system will eventually exceed the ability of the younger work force to support it. At the current rate of increase, in eighteen years social security taxes alone will make up thirty percent of a middle class worker's paycheck.[150]

The Social Security system is unsustainable for another reason. Most people believe that the deductions from their paycheck are going into a giant savings account which will support them in their old age. This is not true. After paying current Social Security recipients, Uncle Sam "borrows" the remaining $110 million daily income by selling government securities to Social Security. The cash derived by the government is used to pay its daily bills and the rising interest on the national debt. However, by selling securities, the government generates even more debt. At the current rate, by 2030 there will be no money to pay Social Security recipients and no surplus to run the government. At that time the middle class taxpayers will be asked to pay all current Social Security benefits, all current government expenses and continue to make payments on the debt.[150]

Elderpower

To what do we owe this national love for aging Social Security recipients at the expense of the young? The answer is political power. The PACs of older Americans are the strongest in the nation and their political power renders them immune to any significant reduction in their unsustainable benefits. One hundred million active members regularly write letters to legislators, work in elections and vote. Their activities are funded through the Older Americans Act of 1965 which provides them with almost a billion federal dollars each year to support their political activities.[150]

Solutions—Social Security

We have several options for dealing with the problem of entitlements for aging Americans. One is to continue with business as usual and allow the social security system to gradually go broke. This will eliminate any future care for the elderly and our national economy will be destroyed when the government no longer receives the $110 million daily "gift" from social security paycheck withholding.[150] Another option is to address the problems and make the necessary changes. Since Americans are now living longer and healthier lives, we can raise the age of retirement. People will work longer, pay more money into the system and take out less. We can also require a "means test" (or needs test) for all government benefits beyond the amount invested and the accrued interest. The needy would receive government support, which was the original intent of the program, and those who have other significant sources of income would not. A means test for Social Security and MediCare, which would limit benefits to those at or above the national median income, would result in a reduction in federal spending of thirty-three percent.[35] Finally, over an extended period of time, we could gradually eliminate Social Security and require people to finance their own retirement with safe, conservative personal investments which would give a higher rate of return than current government securities.

America—For Sale

Let's leave reduced expenditures as a method of dealing with debt and turn to the other option: increasing national income. One controversial method is to sell America to people from other nations. Our country's present and future wealth can be treated as a commodity and sold in the international marketplace. Private wealth includes natural resources, farmland, industry, businesses and buildings. These items are sold by private owners to wealthy foreigners. Government wealth consists of bonds and treasury issues. When these promises of future payment are sold to foreign investors, they provide direct revenue to our government. Then the question becomes how much of America is for sale? In 1988 foreign ownership of private wealth consisted of two percent of our commercial real estate, one percent of this country's farmland and four percent of our corporate stock.[89] Government foreign debt is significantly greater. By 1986 foreigners had invested $300 billion more in U.S. bonds, securities and other assets than we had invested in other countries.[31] As we increase our foreign debt we must also question the long term reliability of the investors. These funds are attracted by America's political and economic security as well as other intangible qualities which give rise to international confidence. These include an educated and motivated work force, quality infrastructure and modern, productive business and industry investing extensively in high technology research and development. Unfortunately these American qualities are in a rapid and continuous state of decline. In the future, if U.S. securities reach an unacceptable level of risk due to our large debt and declining economic security, foreign investors could begin to sell them and take their money out of the American economy. This could lead to a decline in the value of the dollar and accelerated inflation.[173] To solve this problem America must move toward an international balance where the net export of dollars and resources approximate the net imports.[50]

Income Taxes

Other than selling America, the standard method of increasing government revenues has been to raise taxes, usually on income. However, a personal income tax system is supported by citizens only if they believe two things. First the tax is fair; the amount paid is based upon the amount earned and as a result, the burden is equally distributed. Second, the money is fairly and honestly spent to meet the needs of the country. Most Americans rightly believe that our current system has neither of these attributes. Although the wealthy are taxed at a higher rate, politicians, grateful for their campaign contributions have provided a variety of tax loopholes, often through businesses. Thus, the well to do can reduce their taxes significantly. Since the middle class supports the country financially and also believes that they are being taxed unfairly, they use every means available to avoid payment. In 1981 there was an estimated unreported legal income of $150 billion.[183] In an effort to counter this rising revolt, the IRS has hired an army of employees who, at taxpayers expense, attempt to draw more money out of the middle class. Taxpayers also realize that much of their money is wasted. Many blame "welfare cheats"; however, most of the tax money is lost where most of it is spent: in defense, social security, MediCare and government and military pensions.

The problem of unfair taxation can be solved by altering the current complex system. Tax loopholes would be reduced and those remaining would benefit the long term sustainable needs of our country. As business and individuals seek the loopholes, our economy would be directed toward national sustainability.

Jobs in America

Much of America's real wealth is generated by people who work at a job and provide goods or services. However, we are producing fewer goods as our economy becomes dominated by service-oriented businesses. Two-thirds of all American jobs are in areas such as health, finance, entertainment and communications. Many pay low wages and provide few opportunities to increase productivity. A continued reliance on these service industries will prevent America from developing a robust economy.

At the same time many American jobs are disappearing. As we enter a global economy, low skill, mass production jobs are moving to developing countries with cheap labor and few regulations. In an attempt to preserve this work for Americans, we use quotas and tariffs to exclude inexpensive foreign goods and government subsidies to pay American workers more for a product than it is worth in the world marketplace. While this maintains jobs for some Americans, it also increases taxes and the cost of goods and services for American consumers.

Economic Balance

An economic balance must be established and maintained between the "Buy American" bumper sticker economics and the "get more for less" philosophy of capitalism. One solution is to provide initial, limited "start up" government protection for some American business and industry. As they meet required timetables and develop the efficiency and productivity needed to compete in the world marketplace, the support can be terminated. Ultimately however, those American businesses and industries which cannot implement advanced technology and compete with cheaper foreign labor must be "released" to the developing countries.

Corporate Waste and Inefficiency

The major reason American business and industry is in decline is the same reason government does not work very well; waste, inefficiency and corruption also permeate the private sector. Waste in the U.S. economy in 1989 was estimated at 31.9 percent of the GDP. This amounts to $1.7 trillion which could have been directed toward the vital needs of this nation.[22] One result of this waste is low productivity and poor quality products. The cause is often the formal, structured organization of many American businesses which separate employees into divisions and departments. Each worker has a specific job description. Because the type and amount of work varies, some employees work too hard while the accomplishments of others range from little to nothing. In an attempt to maintain individual job security and successfully compete for pay raises and promotions, mutually beneficial information is not shared. The resulting lack of multiple job skills can be disastrous during periods of business decline; it prevents employee transfer and results in layoffs.

An adversarial and often hostile relationship is often maintained between labor and management. The "bosses" attempt to maintain and concentrate their power, and in doing so, isolate themselves from the workers. During lengthy and time-consuming negotiations, both management and labor try to enhance their position at the expense of the other. Management blunts worker demands for higher pay, shorter hours, more fringe benefits, better working conditions and job security. Workers respond with slow downs, strikes or sabotage. Those in charge reciprocate with layoffs, the purchase of automated equipment or plant closures. Collectively this relationship results in fewer quality jobs and higher unemployment. In the end all Americans lose.

A New Approach in American Business and Industry

In order to successfully compete in a global marketplace, we must revitalize our business and industry and provide secure, well-paid jobs for trained technicians and professionals. How can this be accomplished? In the future most of America's industries must make specialized products which are high value, precision engineered and custom tailored to serve a specific market. They will employ rapid change to keep abreast of evolving technologies in computers, machine tools, fiber optics, lasers, biotechnology and robotics. Our future work force must include scientists, engineers, teachers, technical writers and also people skilled in areas such as computer and information science, telecommunications, health care and pollution control.[34]

Continuous education and retraining both on the job and after work maintains and improves a skilled work force. In West Germany, government vouchers are used to pay half of the retraining costs for unemployed workers. The other half is paid by business or industry. It was found that this voucher system paid for itself in reduced unemployment payments and increased job productivity.[154] Raises and promotions will be based on both individual skill and effort and also on overall productivity. A multi-skilled work force will develop as employees teach their skills to each other, enabling the company to quickly change and develop different amounts, sizes or types of products. Job security, productivity, individual income and advancement within the company will increase as the organizational walls which separate labor from management are disassembled. Everyone will be recognized as an important and necessary part of the company and their latent creativity, knowledge and leadership can be encouraged by profit sharing. Employees will be found in small groups, exchanging ideas and working together to improve their products and services. This process will be both exciting and frustrating and lead to some disagreements and failures. But it will also give rise to improvements which benefit all employees. With this new cooperative effort, the work place can become more than a job site. This community of employees will solve other work-related problems such as pollution control, job training, transportation, child and health care as these progressive companies join with other organizations within the surrounding community to provide prosperity, cohesiveness and a safe, enjoyable and healthy place to live.

National Governments, Multinational Corporations and the Global Economy

America must come to grips with a rapidly growing phenomena which affects almost all aspects of our economy: the emergence of worldwide multinational businesses. Historically, nations have been the entity to which most people pledged their allegiance and theoretically derive their social, political and economic security. National business and industry was the economic base and provided employment to citizens. In theory, governments regulated corporations in the best interest of the people and provided support through financial incentives for growth and development. They also produced an educated work force which was often protected from foreign competition through quotas, tariffs or subsidies.

Gradually the multinational corporations assumed a major role in the world's economic systems. Today, because of their enormous size and vast resources, these companies have many advantages. They can quickly adopt different methods to produce advanced products as new world markets are created. Profits are maximized by bringing together all of the necessary production components in any country of their choice. Also, if necessary, they can quickly move goods, capital, technology or management to another country to secure inexpensive labor, and avoid political and financial instability or governmental regulations. Multinationals will even form alliances with their competitors if it enables them to expand their markets and increase their profits.[141]

International stockholders, company executives and some employees benefit from these giant corporations. However, the workers often experience few advantages. In developing countries, the economic power of the multinationals often exceeds that of the national host and a majority of the people in the country are at their mercy. The excessive number of untrained workers provides a large, poor, docile labor force. Thus profits can be maximized by paying minimal wages and doing little or nothing to assist in long term community development or pollution control. In the wealthy, developed countries, these corporations can also threaten national and citizen interests. Educated Americans and their technological skills and products can be transferred by multinationals to any part of the world with no assurance that the benefits will return to our country. This could eventually reduce the role of governments to meeting the needs of these economic giants rather than serving their own people. Economic barriers at national borders including tariffs, subsidies, and import or export restrictions could be eliminated. All countries would then be forced to welcome and encourage any form of economic investment from any corporation and money, goods, services and people could flow unimpeded to countries where the greatest profit is generated. This process is beginning in multinational trade organizations such as the European Economic Community and the Interlined Economy which includes Japan, America and the Western European countries.

Theoretically this process will be financially beneficial for consumers. New global industries will provide the best and cheapest products to all who are able to pay the purchase price with competition forcing corporations to decentralize and focus research and product development on meeting local market demands. Profits will increase by "adding value" to natural resources and tailoring them to meet the needs of individual consumers, resulting in sustained economic growth and improved quality of life for the people of all participating countries.[141]

However, if multinationals become more powerful than national governments and their goal is to increase profits and decrease expenses, who will assume the regulatory and protective functions previously performed by governments? How will individual citizens be protected against dangerous or defective products, pollution or the destruction of natural resources? It is suggested that these functions will be assumed by consumers just as their selective purchases now regulate sales and profits. They will not purchase defective or poor

quality items and as a result irresponsible corporations will be eliminated and their workers will move to other companies.

There are some problems with this concept. Consumers are not
completely informed regarding all of the personal and environmental
product hazards at the time of purchase. They do not know if child
or slave labor was used to produce the item or if ecosystems were
destroyed to secure the necessary raw materials. This theory also
proposes that displaced workers have the option of other jobs of
equal quality. History indicates otherwise. Even with current governmental regulations which attempt to insure worker and consumer
safety and preserve the environment, some companies still maintain
dangerous work places, sell defective products and knowingly pollute the environment. Eliminating government controls and relying
on educated, fully informed and ethical consumers to regulate multinationals would leave no reliable entity to protect the general interests of the people. The net result could be the further concentration
of wealth and power in the hands of the world's elite and a decline in
the quality of life for others. Pushed to its extreme, the concept could
result in a world run by a few wealthy and powerful owners of large
companies. In order to increase profits they would be free to carry
out massive pollution, the depletion of natural resources and the economic enslavement of working people. Some suggest that, to a cer-
tain extent, this is already taking place.

Multinational corporations and international trade are established and will continue to grow and provide the consumer benefits
previously described. However, democratic governments must continue to regulate their activities in the best interest of their citizens.

Economic Philosophy

What then is America's economic future? Before we try to answer this question, lets look at our own personal philosophy. Most
economists would say that we are "econocentric", that economics is
the center of our social universe and all other aspects of our society
orbit around the "econosun". And perhaps they are correct. Most of
us would probably deny that money is the most important item in our
lives; however, we seem to spend most of our time attempting to
secure as much as possible. When asked how much money he
needed, one of the richest men in the world said, "Just a little more

than I have now." Once the money is in hand, our financial transactions express our personal and societal values. The old saying that "philosophy follows finance" is more correctly stated in reverse. As we spend money, we express our values. If America becomes a country in which an informed majority secures the political power needed to determine how our government spends our taxes, our country's future can be determined by the economic philosophy of the voters.

Traditional Economics

What type of economic philosophy will enable us to sustain our current quality of life and also pass it on to our children? First let's look at traditional capitalistic economic theory which is based on continuous growth. As our physical resources such as timber and petroleum decrease, the demand for these scarce resources will drive up the price. The resources will be harvested until they become economically extinct and then substitutes will be developed or discovered.

These traditional economic principles will function for a small population of technologically advanced people who have access to abundant resources. However the unending physical demands of our exploding, primarily non-technological human population are resulting in the rapid extraction of the earth's limited resources. Most renewable resources are decreasing because they are not harvested in a sustainable manner. And if all of the costs of production are calculated (see petroleum costs in the chapter on energy), some of our non-renewable resources are already approaching economic exhaustion. For many of these resources, technology has not developed financially acceptable substitutes, nor will they be produced in the foreseeable future.

Thus, our present economic course is leading us to violate the sacred law of business; capital must not be expended: it must be invested to generate profits. We are consuming our natural resource "capital" rather than living off of the "interest" or profits which is the continued productivity of those resources. This is the result of at least two factors: marketing strategies (advertising) for which we pay $500 annually for each American[91] and our desire to continuously accumulate physical items regardless of the long term impact on our future.

A New Philosophy—Steady State Economics

We must stop treating our earth as if it were a business in a liquidation sale.[50] The solution to our economic problems must begin with a new economic philosophy. Some have already begun this process. They are turning away from the concept summarized by the bumper sticker which reads, "The one who dies with the most toys wins". Many are seeking a lifestyle which emphasizes the quality of relationships with friends and family and work which is meaningful, enjoyable and secure. This idea has its roots in our history. Earlier, personal worth was measured by integrity, honesty, skill and hard work. Some religious groups such as the Quakers and Amish have always lived lives of voluntary simplicity. From these groups has come the concept of a sustainable society, the ecological equivalent of the Golden Rule. Each generation leaves the earth in a state which allows future generations to enjoy the same quality of life. They rightfully assume that the future of humankind depends upon our ability to limit our consumption of resources and the pollution of our planet.[91]

Can a sustainable lifestyle be incorporated into, and become the basis for, a capitalistic economy? There is a form of capitalism which does not rely upon endless growth and the over consumption of resources. It is termed steady state economics.[50] This system is based upon the concept of sustainable development; developing products and improving the lives of people within the limits of sustained resources and stable human populations.[54] Development increases the quality of life through technology, information and education. Necessary goods and services increase through improved efficiency and productivity and fewer, longer lasting items are produced. This results in lower rates of resource consumption and less pollution.

If steady state economics is implemented, the strategy will vary between the wealthy developed countries of the "North" or northern hemisphere and the poor developing countries of the "South": the southern hemisphere. The North will reduce its consumption of natural resources by increasing energy efficiency and reducing waste and pollution. Taxing resource depletion will encourage efficiency and the restoration of our natural capital. However, in the poor

South, economic growth must continue, with the assistance of the North, to allow for the emergence of sustainable agriculture, business, industry education and health care. With investment, technology, training, education and loan forgiveness the South will be able to build and support their own economies, lift themselves out of poverty and reduce disruptive migration to the developed countries. To insure continued success, these programs must also be accompanied by a reduction in the present human population through a massive decrease in birthrates.

CHAPTER FIVE

FAMILIES, COMMUNITIES, CRIME AND ILLEGAL DRUGS

The "Good Old Days"

Our parents and grandparents still talk about "the good old days" in America. Typically, marriages were for the life of the couple and two-parent families were the social center and stabilizing force in our society. Towns were comparatively small and communities were uniform and close knit. Residents knew each other and there was a code of ethics and behavior which was accepted and followed by almost everyone. Doors were left unlocked and there was a real feeling of safety and security within the community. Those who violated the law were usually caught and punished.

Social Change

Gradually our society began to change. Population increased and many towns became large cities. People became transitory and as extended families and cohesive communities decreased, private organizations and governmental institutions attempted to assume their role. Many pursued individual rights and formed networks with others who had the same interests. Often, people no longer felt the need to know those who lived around them or participate in community activities. Many relinquished the role of protection to professional law enforcement.

Present Families and Communities

Today relationships which were previously considered permanent have often become transitory. Almost half of all marriages end in divorce and many fathers do not assist in the financial support of their children or former wives. Single parent families also come into being as young sexually active, men and women are either unable or unwilling to secure and use contraceptives. Some girls and women have abortions but many keep their children and the total burden of parent, home keeper and wage earner falls onto the mother. Many single mothers manage with great difficulty to establish a functioning family and successfully raise their children. But others fail. Assistance is often inadequate to secure minimal food, housing and health care. Without these basic life requirements and the needed social support, education and job opportunities necessary to break out of the welfare cycle, they cannot join the working class and secure the American dream. With little hope of a better life, these women often become poverty stricken, isolated, homeless and vulnerable to physical attack or drug addiction. Many of their children experience even greater suffering. In 1988 an estimated 100,000 fetuses were abused in the womb by mothers who were addicted to cocaine. Each year, thousands of women bear babies with fetal alcohol syndrome. In some parts of New York City more than ten percent of the children are born with a death sentence; they are HIV positive.[31] The children of poverty also receive an inferior education, are often physically or sexually abused and the incidence of malnutrition and preventable disease approaches that of third world countries. As a result of these tragedies, hundreds of thousands of children and teenagers do not receive the needed love, support and discipline required for normal development and socialization. Many drop out of school and without access to adequate employment or social position, they are added to the increasing welfare rolls or join the youth gang subculture.

The loss of functional families and communities is not only this country's greatest social disaster, it is also a threat to our political and economic stability. Families and communities are the glue which holds our society together and as they fail mutually agreed upon values are abandoned. Other vital components of our society then begin to crumble, business, industry, law and order and even truly representative government.

Solutions

Where families and communities are malfunctioning, they must be supported and where they have been destroyed they will be rebuilt. The "traditional" family made up of two parents and one or more children is still the mainstay of our society however the growing number of single parent families need equal status and support. Single parents require access to an education or job training. They often need incentives including loans and child care which can be provided by competitive private or nonprofit groups. Parents will earn partial loan forgiveness when they become successfully employed. This will enable them to become self-fulfilling, socially functioning, wage-earning and tax-paying citizens.

Every child must have the opportunity to be a member of a "family" and eventually become an adult who can function within the norms of our society. The vast, scattered army of underage runaways, throwaways and orphans can be matched with state approved "families". The "parents" will be those with proven, successful experience in raising children or other adults trained in the necessary skills. These families can be under contract with the State and operated as a private or nonprofit enterprise. They will have specific objectives. Children and young people can be expected to attend school or work, obey the law, avoid illegal drugs, not conceive a child and support other members of the group. Just as employees receive a bonus if the business succeeds, successful families will earn annual cash awards. This will encourage cooperation, unity and mutual support among the members. Not all of these families will succeed and some members will move to other more compatible groups. Those who continue to violate the rules of society will be transferred into the criminal justice system. Funding to support these new families will be derived from the money formerly spent on these children when they were on welfare or in the criminal justice system.

As families are supported or rebuilt, small internal "communities" can be formed within cities or towns. They will organize Neighborhood Watch groups to prevent crime and cooperatives to provide child care, support groups, transportation, neighborhood restoration and beautification. Financial incentives will encourage participation in these community activities. They will include property tax discounts for home owners and for landlords who will be required to pass tax reductions on to tenants. To insure participation in the higher levels of government, these "communities" will elect representatives to attend city council meetings and present the views of their members.

Crime in America

As families and communities are rebuilt we must also address the problem of crime. In 1990 there were approximately 23,000 homicides in America.[31] Violent crime is increasing and extending from the poor inner cities to middle and upper class neighborhoods. Inundated by a barrage of newspaper and television accounts of local violence, many Americans no longer feel safe or secure on the streets or in their homes. They believe they are potential victims and live in fear of the loss of their property or physical assault. In an attempt to defend themselves, they fortify their homes, schools and work places with bars on the windows and doors, alarm systems and perimeter defenses which include high fences with razor wire, guard dogs or armed security officers. Looking out through the bars of their self-made prisons, many fearfully survey the dangerous area beyond. They have isolated themselves from the group protection of neighbors and often become the prey of criminals. Their total abdication of involvement in community crime control to a professional police force has given this enormous task to a small group of dedicated people who are hampered by budget constraints, legal limitations and bureaucratic paperwork.

Youth Gangs

In neighborhoods where there is an absence of strong families, effective community leadership and sufficient police protection, the youth gangs often move in to fill the power vacuum. This extended family of peers provides its members with strong leadership, protection, support and companionship. In return it demands total obedience, loyalty and sacrifice. The gang maintains its physical and economic power through assault, robbery, burglary, rape, murder and the sale of illegal drugs. Prestige and profits increase as gangs spread throughout the country to franchise well-organized crime and drug distribution networks. In their battles for turf and power, many are now armed with automatic weapons. Some have greater firepower than the local police and large sections of our cities, particularly at night, are under their control. They terrorize citizens and then melt back into massive urban slums where, out of fear of ambush, police often refuse to follow. When riot conditions are precipitated and law enforcement is temporarily overwhelmed, they are free to roam at will and burn, maim and kill. If current conditions persist, state governments could frequently be forced to call out the national guard to support local police. Because the guard is inadequately trained and supplied to fight an urban guerrilla war, the Federal government will increasingly be required to provide the expensive support of regular army troops.

The Court System

The courts are perhaps the weakest link in our criminal justice system. They are almost incapacitated by the enormous number of criminal complaints, primarily drug related and against young urban males. In an attempt to make the system function, judges are forced to move a large number of cases through the courts in a short period of time. Plea bargaining, and the resulting reduction in punishment for a crime, is an attempt to expose criminals to some justice as an alternative to a long expensive trial and possible acquittal. Since the juvenile justice system is not designed to deal with major crimes, children are often recruited by older thugs to engage in drug trafficking, robbery and murder. Thus the young criminals, and often their adult employers, enjoy the benefits of crime without the threat of serious punishment. When offenders are caught, it is often months or years before they come to trial. These delays result in the intimidation and loss of witnesses and freedom for criminals.

Solutions

With the reestablishment of families and communities and the implementation of effective drug control programs, which will be described shortly, crime and the number of court cases will be reduced. Also, community arbitration and small claims courts will be expanded to deal with minor offenses. With fewer cases, accused adults can be placed on a time track whereby they pass through the various required steps of the system without delay. Two major changes can be initiated in the juvenile justice process; a redesigned mechanism for the rapid and effective disposition of major, violent crimes and rehabilitation programs for those involved in first or minor offenses.

Prisons

Despite the fact that many criminals are either released without imprisonment or are serving shortened sentences, world wide our country has the dubious distinction of confining the highest percentage of its citizens behind bars. One million Americans are incarcerated and seventy-five percent of those were convicted on drug related charges. Yet our crime rate and rampant drug use continue to increase.[127]

In an attempt to maintain adequate security and living conditions, prisons have become more costly to construct and maintain. It is now more expensive to send a young person to prison than to educate them at Harvard or Yale. Still our multimillion dollar prison building program cannot keep up with the increasing number of inmates and murder and riots are commonplace in these over-crowded institutions. Because most of our funds must be used to build and maintain prisons and employ guards, there is little money available for counseling, rehabilitation and job training and few prisoners are converted into law-abiding citizens. The only training most inmates receive is in the informal "crime schools" which are conducted by older, hardened criminals. When prisoners are released, often prematurely due to over-crowded conditions, they are usually less prepared to be honest citizens than when they were first incarcerated and many again commit crimes.

Solutions

Lets examine some answers to these complex and expensive problems. First we can reduce the cost of prisons. Following the pattern of the Texas State Prison system, all prisons can become self-supporting. Prisoners can carry out much of the construction, maintenance and operations. Those activities which cannot be performed by prisoners will be financed by profits generated in prison farms and industries.

We also need to reexamine sentencing laws. We must realize that many criminals should not be released. Repeat offenders and violent criminals who cannot be rehabilitated must remain in self-supporting prisons. However, others who are convicted of crimes against people or property, and who are candidates for rehabilitation should receive counseling, education and job training. Many first time convicted criminals who are not yet hardened can eventually become law-abiding, productive and self-supporting members of society. If and when these prisoners are judged to be rehabilitated and also have the necessary job skills to gain employment in the community, they can be released from prison and begin to serve a second or external portion of their sentence. Wearing leg-secured radio tracking devices and monitored at all times by law enforcement agencies, these employed prisoners will be allowed to move only from home to their work and to counseling sessions. During other hours they will be under house arrest. As self and family supporting workers, their salary above the amount needed to pay for necessities can be placed in a fund to compensate victims of crime and assist in the support of the criminal justice system. Granted more personal freedom or a reduced sentence if they exhibit measurable attitudinal and behavioral changes, their external monitored sentence will be terminated when they are judged to be fully rehabilitated. Monitoring will continue while on parole and final release granted only after an extended period of successful citizenship. Those who fail to meet these conditions will be imprisoned.

Those convicted of crimes which do not harm persons or property will not be imprisoned. Receiving an initial, external sentence they can be monitored and required to follow the previously described procedures for convicted criminals including self and family support, compensation of victims and support of the criminal justice system.

Drugs

America has approximately six million cocaine users, 500,000 heroin addicts and twenty million who smoke marijuana. Most of the crime in America is associated with illegal drugs. In 1988 between twenty-eight and forty million drug related crimes were committed in the U.S. They included drug use and trafficking and also violent crimes against innocent people to secure money for drug purchase. The arrest rate for these crimes is estimated at only two to three percent.[35]

Our major strategy against illegal drugs is a "war" to eliminate drugs and drug use with massive law enforcement programs. "Military campaigns" include attempts to halt drugs at several points; the growing of drug producing plants, the smuggling of drugs into America and the distribution, sale and use of illegal drugs in this country. The annual cost, excluding prisons, of this war is forty-two billion dollars. As a result of an increase in the number of law enforcement officers and prosecutors, arrests and convictions have increased and we now have approximately 500,000 drug related "prisoners of war".

With this tremendous expenditure of money and effort, are we winning the war on drugs? When law enforcement officers, probation officials and those in the courts are asked this question, the answer is almost always the same, an unqualified no. In one survey of state and local prosecutors, two-thirds said that despite the heroic efforts of the police and the courts, there was little or no reduction in the supply or use of drugs in their area. Will more money enable us to win the war on drugs? Under current conditions, none of those interviewed thought that drugs could be eliminated using current strategies regardless of the funds expended.[35]

Solutions

America is losing the war on drugs because we are fighting a business with an estimated profit of $100 billion annually. This is twice the amount of money used to purchase petroleum for our industrialized society.[35] Financially, the drug trade is an ideal national and multinational business venture. Driven by a constantly growing consumer demand, the restricted supply of inexpensive illegal drugs can be sold at an enormous profit. An initial investment of $175 in speed (methamphetamine) will generate a street profit of $32,000. Drugs have other marketing advantages. They can be easily hidden and transported and then diluted to increase their retail value. A relatively small percentage of the profits can be used to bribe some of the police, judges and politicians in any country. When this fails, small armies of criminals with sophisticated weapons can be employed to protect the trade. The potential labor force needed to support this booming business is enormous. There is a large number of affluent, middle class or poor young people seeking high wages and short hours.

In order to win the war on drugs we must eliminate the profits. This can be done with legislation which will provide at least three different strategies. The first will be directed against those criminals who are physically dependent upon illegal drugs. Their crimes include trafficking, prostitution, mugging, robbery, burglary and the murder of innocent Americans. Typically these crimes are not committed as a result of taking illegal drugs. They are perpetrated to secure the money needed to purchase the addictive drugs. These addicts can be registered and provided with federally funded, community-based drug administration facilities similar to our present methadone clinics for heroin addicts. Here physicians can administer drugs at no cost to those who are addicted. Users will also be encouraged to participate in rehabilitation programs with financial, social and personal incentives which include training in job skills and family relationships. Many will stop using drugs, however, as with any rehabilitation program, some will fail. Those who are not rehabilitated will continue to receive drugs at no charge. A similar program functions successfully in England. Here physicians prescribe free drugs to registered addicts. The prescriptions are filled in a pharmacy and self administered at home. Most addicts work and live fairly normal lives and many are gradually rehabilitated. There has been a marked decline in drug related crime, new addicts and the cost of health care which was formerly required for treatment of infection from contaminated street drugs.

A different strategy will be used with the second category of drug users, the employed adult who is a noncriminal, non addicted, recreational participant. Since drug use decreases productivity in business and industry and may endanger other employees, it should be reduced and hopefully eliminated. Negative advertising campaigns will stress the social unacceptability of drug use. Employees who exhibit poor job performance which could be caused by drug use will be required to undergo testing. Users will be moved to a position where job performance is not affected by "off the job" drug use and undergo rehabilitation. Those who are rehabilitated will return to their original position. Others who fail rehabilitation will remain at their new job and register as an addict. Business productivity and profits should increase and absenteeism and accidents decline as employee drug use is reduced. These programs can be financed with the increased profits generated by a more productive work force.

The third target group is children and young people. Well funded anti-drug educational programs in schools will be extensive and mandatory. These programs have proven effective in establishing values and reducing drug use later in life. Voluntary drug testing programs with various incentives for participation will be carried out in schools with those who test positive undergoing anonymous rehabilitation. These education and testing programs can be funded with a small portion of the forty-two billion dollars we are currently spending to finance our war on drugs.

As a result of these various programs, the illegal drug trade can be significantly reduced and most of the remaining dealers apprehended, tried and imprisoned. With much of the crime in America eliminated, law enforcement officials can concentrate on non drug-related violations. The justice system will begin to function in a normal manner and as prison populations decline, we can finally win the war on drugs and also save billions of dollars.

CHAPTER SIX

EDUCATION

Future Classroom

Conversation subsides as students from a variety of economic, racial and cultural backgrounds enter a classroom which is clean, safe and well equipped. This theoretical class begins the day with large group instruction conducted by the teacher. The class is then divided into small clusters of students which are directed by trained aides. One group prepares for an upcoming examination, while in another area students view an educational television program. Some work on written reports or computer-assisted instructional programs. Because educational research tells us that students learn in a variety of ways and at different rates, they are grouped by learning style and ability level. A team effort is encouraged, and students help and support each other. Grouping facilitates learning; however, all students are allowed to progress at their own rate and as a result all are successful.

Student success is frequently reported to parents who are encouraged to reinforce progress at home. Because some parents do not support their child's education, abundant recognition and awards are given in class. Students are constantly reminded of the importance of school. It enables them to understand and appreciate their world and is their ticket to a good job and financial security. Learning is also challenging, interesting and, in many cases, fun. But even under optimum conditions, some students misbehave. Minor troublemakers are sentenced to trash pickup during recess or lunch period, a penalty which usually results in rapid behavioral reform.

Those who continue to disrupt learning are removed from the classroom for counseling or discipline.

Present Schools

What is the current condition of our educational system? For the most part, it is failing to meet the needs of our children and our nation. Top-heavy bureaucracies have become embedded at federal, state and local levels. They siphon money away from classrooms to produce endless, required surveys and studies which do little to improve learning. Those school administrators who are genuinely concerned about the quality of classroom teaching and learning are often unable to provide effective assistance to teachers. They are burdened with reduced budgets, personnel problems and overcrowded classrooms. The security of their schools is disrupted by gangs which deal drugs and protect turf. Frequently principals are forced to organize schools not as educational institutions, but as fenced, student storage facilities.

Both rookie and veteran teachers are often faced with conditions which make instruction impossible. New, bright-eyed, energetic and idealistic teachers are slammed into our modern blackboard jungles. Many are unprepared and underpaid and half of these new instructors leave the classroom within seven years.[36] Older teachers may adapt by psychologically entrenching themselves in an attempt to survive until early retirement. As a result of these conditions, there will be a shortage of a million teachers by 1995.[37]

Faced with this failing educational system, one million students leave American schools each year without graduating. During their lifetime, these dropouts will collectively lose $240 billion each year in potential earnings.[36] Many of these young Americans, who should be preparing to run our country, are becoming either parasites or predators on other members of our society.

Others, who remain in our ailing schools, will graduate without the basic skills and advanced knowledge necessary for success in our modern technological society. This lack of a quality educational system in our country is constantly revealed in comparative test scores. For instance, America's high school seniors finish dead last when their test results are compared with those of the high school seniors in eight other industrialized countries. Japanese high school graduates, when compared with their counterparts in America, have the equivalent of two additional years of education.

High Schools

American high schools emphasize a precollege curriculum and many bright, motivated students are adequately prepared for higher education. However, most high school graduates do not want or need a four-year college education. Only fifteen percent of the positions in the future American work force will require a baccalaureate degree.[36] Thus, our modern high schools have few classes and little practical guidance to meet the needs of a majority of their students. Without a true picture of future employment requirements or the classes needed to gain the necessary skills and knowledge, many of these young people find no relevance in their education and they simply walk away from school.

Students who remain in the system often lack parental discipline and support or realistic future goals. Many take the minimum number of classes and study as little as possible. They either participate in extracurricular activities, work at part time jobs or just "hang out." Their education prepares them only for menial, low paying jobs.

Industry and Education

In an attempt to compensate for the failure of our high schools, large companies such as IBM, Ford and Xerox are spending $210 billion per year on employee education and training.[36] This money must be taken from research and development budgets and the other urgent needs of business and industry. Most small companies have limited financial resources and are unable to offer any employee training. Business leaders rightfully claim that our present national economic decline is directly related to the poor quality of American education.

The Bridge

In order to provide a majority of our students with an understanding of our world and successful employment in a technological work force, it is necessary to build a bridge between the classroom and the work place. Students, parents and teachers must know the educational requirements for the future American job market. This can be accomplished with videotaped programs which include both interviews with leaders of business and industry, and tours of facilities which describe the modern equipment and required skills necessary for employment.

Future Schools and Employment

Students will find that most future quality jobs will emerge in the technical fields, the service sector, or in information science. They and their parents can then see the necessity of rigorous classes in both high school and technical or community college in the following areas; specialized skills, traditional general education, communications, information access and critical thinking. In order to provide this type of relevant education, teachers and administrators will develop new courses and curricula. This includes basic classes in the two languages of our society, English and mathematics, followed by specialized course work and on-the-job internship programs for course credit. As the quality of education is improved, it is important that the quantity also increase. While American students attend high school an average 6.5 hours per day for 180 days, Japanese students receive a superior education due partly to an eight-hour day and a 240-day school year.[36] Finally, when American students complete their education in these redesigned schools, they will be able to move directly into the positions for which they have been trained. Continuing education in the work place can enable employees to advance to higher levels in their present field or to move into other related areas.

Elementary Schools

Let us turn to the heart of American education, the elementary school. This is where basic skills and attitudes are established. Bright, eager and energetic children often enter our schools only to find crowded classrooms with insufficient books and supplies. Typically they are placed in large classes with others of the same age where a wide range of subject matter knowledge, English proficiency and behavioral problems exist. Caring, overworked teachers attempt to instruct all of these children in basic skills, critical thinking, acceptable behavior and moral values. In order to be effective with such a diverse group, a teacher must attempt to instruct students in all subjects at multiple levels. Since this is an impossible task, many teach to the average student. The results are predictable: the bright students are bored and lose interest and those who need more time or assistance continue to fail.

Inner City Schools

Our educational problems are most severe in our inner cities. Soon twenty-five percent of all American children under six years of age will be in poverty and most of these kids live in our cities.[31] For many, their only stable environment is the classroom. They come with hope and a faint but detectable sparkle in their eyes. School is new, interesting, exciting and fun. Elementary school teachers, who have not been ground down by our current educational system, are constantly awed and inspired by their flexibility, openness and desire to learn. But these kids face a difficult future. Many are exposed to crime and drugs in their families or in local communities. Some suffer from disease, malnutrition or physical abuse, and if present conditions persist, their quality of life will continue to decline. Failure to address their educational and social needs will push them into expanding welfare systems and jails rather than toward a rewarding position in the future work force of a successful America.

Future Schools

How can we restore both our elementary schools and the other levels of our educational system to meet the needs of our country and fulfill the dreams of our children? First, it is imperative that we change the philosophy of our school systems. Our first priority will be to optimize learning, and all other activities will center around this goal. What should students know in order to lead productive, prosperous and enjoyable lives in our modern society? Studies indicate that American students need an understanding of the basic, traditional subjects, creative and critical thinking, technological skills and modern systems of communication and information access. It is also important to have an appreciation of family, community, human culture and international relations in order to function successfully in their own multicultural society and in the global village which will be a part of their future.

Future Teachers

Every classroom needs a successful teacher. If we expect to attract highly qualified people to the teaching profession, we must offer competitive salaries. Teachers wages will be comparable to those in other professions which require the same amount of education and expertise. Also, the requirements for state certification in both academic subjects and teaching methods should be upgraded. Continuing education programs for teachers can be designed by teachers and educational experts to insure that they are relevant to the real problems in the classroom. In order to facilitate successful learning, a skilled teacher needs resources. This includes standard classroom teaching materials and also the equipment common to our technological society—computers and educational television. Community representatives from business, industry and the arts can be called upon to provide curricular enrichment and career guidance. Teachers must also be able to prevent disruptive behavior. They will have the support of a referral system which enables them to send students with problems for counseling or to special classes.

To improve student learning, teachers will be evaluated periodically. However, to insure that the process is effective, teachers will be involved in the development, design and implementation of their own evaluation. This will include an assessment of student learning which can be measured with a variety of standardized examinations in order to prevent cultural or language bias. Quality teaching also includes the development of improved teaching techniques and advanced educational course work. As in any business or profession, successful teachers will receive significant raises. Marginal teachers will be required to participate in special educational programs which enable them to become good instructors. Those who do not improve will be fired. As a result of these procedures, all schools can be staffed with effective teachers.

Optimum Learning For All

Quality teachers will develop successful teaching strategies: designing educational programs around the new neurological and behavioral research which delves into the learning process. According to Harvard researcher Howard Gardner, there are as many as seven different types of intelligence. Each appears to operate independently and reach an optimum at a specific time in one's life. Thus different methods of teaching are required to maximize learning for individual students.[34] Simple testing can determine each child's optimal learning pattern and appropriate teaching methods will then be used. Learning groups of various sizes can be formed based upon the needs of children and the skills of different teachers. The possible combinations of teaching techniques and student learning strategies available are almost endless. The rate of instruction is also critical. Computers can now diagnose student learning problems and generate individualized instructional programs which allow students to learn successfully at their own speed.

Teachers need to be involved in instruction; however, they should also function as learning managers as they design and evaluate new teaching methods for individual students. Initially some teachers will view these changes with concern. But most are talented, flexible and innovative. This is a requirement for survival in today's schools. If instructors are encouraged to be risk-takers and to develop new teaching methods in their classrooms, exciting and successful learning will emerge.

Organized for Learning

Our traditional concept of the school day and the school year will be altered. Because the parents of most children work, schools and private industry can develop a system of child care and educational preschool for all children during the entire work day. This is not just a convenience for parents; it is an important investment in the future of this country. A follow-up study of young adults who, as children, attended preschool for only one year determined that this group had a significantly higher number of high school graduates and twice the expected number attended college.[31]

The method of grouping students in classes will also change. They have traditionally been placed in grades based upon age because of their similar social levels and experiences. However, we know that children of the same age have a variety of skills and learning abilities and for this reason it is impossible to effectively teach all of them at the same time. The Corporate Community School in Chicago solved the problem by eliminating grades. Students move through the subject matter at their own pace regardless of their age.

They progress on to a higher level only when they have mastered the current subject matter.[34] Our schools must also simulate our real society with its variety of cultures, languages, races and religions. During some sessions, students can be organized into heterogeneous groups with others who possess varied skills and are from different backgrounds.   In these "mixed groups," students will learn problem-solving techniques, discuss social, moral and ethical questions and then design solutions to current problems using their varied academic, social, cultural and language skills.

Future Administration

It is imperative that expensive, top-down educational organization be replaced with a system which gives teachers and principals control of their schools and responsibility for student learning. This strategy is termed school-based or site-based management. Control of schools includes the distribution of financial resources and also the determination of the type and number of staff. Since learning increases when all participants "buy into" the system, students sign contracts which require acceptable behavior, completion of assignments and a sincere endeavor to learn. Teachers can also ask parents to sign an agreement which requires them to monitor and reinforce their child's learning at home. Parents will be invited to serve on school advisory boards and become a vital part of the educational process. Half of the schools in Miami, Florida have adopted site-based management and learning has increased measurably. Both teacher and student morale are high and there is a new pride in the schools.

Financial Support

To insure universal access to a quality education, all schools require sufficient funding. Two aspects of educational financing must be considered: the equal distribution of money and the total amount needed to provide a quality education. Presently funds are unequally distributed; schools in wealthy communities receive more money than those in poor areas. This inequity can be resolved by dividing all of the money derived from federal, state and local governments equally among all of the students in the state. There will be some exceptions; varying amounts are needed at different grade levels and additional funds will go to those with disabilities and English language problems. This new distribution will not rob wealthy districts of current funds; all schools will receive increased financial support. The additional money can be secured in part by eliminating waste, inefficiency, fraud and corruption at all levels along with the expensive administrative bureaucracy. Site-based management will redirect most of our current educational dollars into the classroom. Once educators have designed a successful, cost-effective system and demonstrated this to the public in model schools, taxpayers will provide additional funds. The American people know that their quality of life is supported by an educated citizenry, and they will provide financial support when teachers accurately indicate the amount needed to accomplish the task.

To insure that public funds will provide equal access to a quality education, these monies will be distributed to schools through parent-held educational vouchers, negotiable only in state-certified public or private schools. In order to maintain community-based education, all children will be guaranteed access to their local school. If desirable schools exceed an optimum enrollment, they can be divided internally into separate institutions or duplicated in other areas. All schools will be periodically accredited to insure that they are successfully teaching a state approved curriculum with certificated teachers. State testing, using a variety of standardized, cultural and language sensitive examinations, will measure the progress of individual student learning. Schools can also be evaluated for other qualities, safety, security, innovative teaching and interesting and exciting learning experiences. The general results of these accreditation studies will be available to parents and children to assist them in selecting their school.

Quality Education For All

Those schools which are successfully educating children will attract students and be enlarged or replicated. Those which are unsuccessful will experience decreasing enrollments and be reorganized or restaffed and modeled after those which are growing. As a result of these changes all publicly funded schools can provide a continually improving, quality education.

In order to rescue our educational system, it is necessary to make a national commitment to change and improvement. This will include redesigned schools centered around successful student learning with quality educators, curricula and facilities. If we take this step, all of America's schools can be of the quality described in the mythical school at the beginning of the chapter.

CHAPTER SEVEN

HEALTH CARE

The Problem

The cost of medical care in America has doubled in the last seven years. We are now spending two billion dollars per day, which amounts to 12.3 percent of our GNP. At the current rate of increase, in ten years we will be spending $1.6 trillion per year and in twenty years one-third of our national resources will be expended for health care.[35] Even with this tremendous increase in expenditures, adequate treatment is currently unavailable to many Americans. In response to rising costs, many private insurance companies have reduced coverage and raised premiums and co-payments. As a result, policy holders who are sick see a physician less frequently and delayed treatment often results in serious and expensive illness. Many no longer have health insurance because they have either lost their job or their employer cannot afford the premiums. One out of nine working American families, most employed by small business, now have no coverage.

In increasing numbers, uninsured Americans are turning to the government for help. But as funds are cut, administrators are tightening entrance requirements and reducing services. Medicaid, which is designed to provide health care to the poor, gives minimal assistance to only forty percent of those who are legally eligible. Financially strapped private hospitals and clinics attempt to avoid caring for those on Medicaid and also uninsured patients who cannot hope to pay their enormous medical bills. Illnesses become progressively worse as these patients are either turned away or shuttled from one health care facility to another. When they finally become very sick, they are admitted to over-crowded, understaffed government hospitals or clinics where their injury or illness requires prolonged and expensive treatment.

Due to a variety of factors, including reduced access to health care, the life expectancy of the average American is shorter than the average citizen in fourteen other industrialized nations, and we have the highest infant mortality rate in the developed world.[154] Declining health occurs primarily among the working middle class and poor. It reduces adult productivity in the work place and unhealthy children often do poorly in school. If this situation continues, a large number of Americans will become both physically and educationally debilitated.

General Solutions

In order to reverse this trend, it is mandatory that we make two major changes in our country's health care system. First reduce the cost of this care and second, extend medical services to those who currently receive little or no assistance. These proposed changes appear to be contradictory. Can we treat more people for less money? We can if we are willing to change our approach to maintaining good health.

Prevention

The most effective and least expensive method of reducing the cost and increasing the availability of health care is preventative medicine. If we prevent illness, we have eliminated most of its cost. The most effective methods of preventing disease are changes in harmful lifestyles, early detection, education and insuring patient compliance with the physicians directions. Most of the illness in America is self-inflicted and changes in lifestyles can prevent these disorders. Rather than charging everyone for the unhealthful behavior of a few, those who participate will pay for the treatment of their self-induced illnesses. Financial disincentives can include user health taxes on items and behaviors which result in poor health. Since trauma is the leading cause of injury and death in Americans under thirty-five years of age, a tax can be placed on consumer goods and activities which contribute to these injuries. The amount of this tax can be determined by studies which identify the cost of individual injuries. The greater the cost of treatment, the higher the tax. For instance, automobiles without automatically locking seat belts and air bags will be taxed at a higher rate than those which do have these safety devices. Because cardiovascular disease and cancer are still the leading causes of death in Americans over thirty-five, a health tax should be placed on the production and purchase of tobacco and foods high in saturated fats and cholesterol. A large increase in taxes will result in decreased consumption and a decline in the incidence of disease, disability, hospitalization and premature death. A change in the behaviors which give rise to cardiovascular disease could prevent illness in 11.5 million people and 6.5 million premature deaths. It would also prevent the loss of 260 billion dollars in business productivity in the next twenty-five years.[146]

Early detection during required, periodic physical examinations enables physicians to treat disorders before they become major and expensive illnesses. Education is also a significant deterrent to disease. Extensive and mandatory educational programs in schools would encourage proper diet, teach strategies for maintaining mental health and preventing accidents and drug use. Inoculation against all infectious diseases will reduce future illness. All pregnant women need prenatal care and education in both maternal health and infant and child care. This will prevent many disorders which originate in the fetus or in early childhood.

HIV Infection

This disease has moved into the general population and now infects at least one million Americans. Faced with an inevitable increase, we still fail to apply the standard public health procedures which are used to control any contagious, epidemic disease. Along with preventative measures such as extensive public education and condom distribution, we must determine who is infected by creating an environment in which those at risk will volunteer for testing. This can be accomplished by insuring that those who are determined to be infected will not face political or economic discrimination. Access to test results should be confined to health officials. Those who test positive can receive special education in the prevention of HIV trans-

mission, health care including currently available drug therapy and
psychological assistance through support groups.

Contraception

The large number of unwanted conceptions are a major health
care expense. The medical costs, which are often paid by the public,
involve either an abortion or care for the mother and infant. Many
unwanted children are on welfare and are provided a meager exist-
ence. This pattern is often perpetuated in the next generation.

The frenzied debate between "right to life" and "pro choice"
advocates disguises the real problem. The moral, medical and social
cost of either an abortion or the birth of an unwanted (and often un-
loved) child arise from either the lack of or failed contraception. Because we now have a variety of safe, convenient and inexpensive
contraceptive techniques, unwanted pregnancy and abortion can be
significantly reduced. This can be accomplished by providing education to all sexually mature teenagers and adults and a choice of free
or inexpensive contraceptives to all who are sexually active.

Genetic Disease

Another pressing American health problem which can be alle-
viated by either education or early detection is the increasing incidence of severe genetic disease. We have developed new and
effective treatments for some of these disorders including the genetically engineered production of insulin for those with diabetes. However, we have no cure for over 3,000 different genetic disorders and
we spend millions of dollars to treat these patients. Many who are
afflicted are able to survive and often lead a productive life with the
harmful genes. However, if they do not limit their reproductive activities, the number of very sick children will increase with each generation. Severe genetic disease can be reduced in future generations
by identifying those who now carry the defective genes and providing them with education and alternatives. This can include genetic
counseling, the option of abortion of a fetus with a severe disorder or
voluntary sterilization of affected adults coupled with preferential
access to adoption services. These programs would satisfy the cou-
ples' need for normal, healthy children.

Following Physician Directions

Another major barrier to good health is the failure of patients to follow the directions of their physician. Often prescribed medications are either not taken by patients or are incorrectly self-administered. Patient follow up through telephone calls or by mail will reduce this problem.

Cost—Benefit Treatment

Modern medical technology has provided us with dramatic, newsworthy and often miraculous procedures such as organ transplants and MRI (magnetic resonance imaging). The criteria for determining which patients will have access to these enormously expensive procedures are often economic; those with sufficient health care coverage are served. These high technology procedures are necessary and desirable however access should be limited to those who will experience an extensive period of health as a result of their use.

Another group of patients which receive a large share of our health care funds are those with terminal diseases or disorders and little chance of continued quality of life. Examples include patients with advanced cancer or AIDS and the elderly who are nearing the end of their life with multiple, major illnesses. Forty percent of the money expended for individual health care is used for acute medical treatment in the last five years of life.[33] Often this does nothing more than prolong a painful and agonizing death.

Just as we carefully plan the major aspects of our life, including our career, home, family, investments and retirement, while we are in good health we can also design a plan which will allow us to die with dignity. As an incentive, a reduction in health care premiums could be provided to those who prepare a "living will" which excludes the use of expensive, non-productive, death postponing treatments as they approach the end of life. If individuals choose to do so, they should also be allowed to select a painless procedure to voluntarily terminate their life when they are near death.

Other Reforms

A variety of other reforms in the current medical system will reduce our health care costs. Estimates of unnecessary medical procedures ordered by physicians run as high as twenty percent of all medical treatment. This is an approximate annual expenditure of $132 billion.[33] These expensive, diagnostic and therapeutic techniques can be limited or capped based upon actual patient need and potential benefit.

Fraud

In the health care system, as in any industry, there is fraud. The annual cost of this white collar crime is estimated at $75 billion.[33] Some doctors and hospitals bill insurance companies or the government for procedures which are not performed. Other physicians are involved in conflict of interest arrangements. They refer their patients to clinical laboratories, physical therapy units or rehabilitation centers which they own. These abuses can be prevented by paying physicians a salary or a flat fee rather than basing their income on the number of tests or procedures they carry out. HMOS have initiated this process and have reduced the cost of traditional medical service delivery by as much as seventeen percent without an increase in overall mortality rates.

Record Keeping

The cost of record keeping for American health care is estimated at $90 billion per year. A single standardized form for all insurance and government fees could save about $20 billion annually. Standardized procedures and integrated computer systems could also reduce the cost of record keeping.[33]

Malpractice Insurance

The cost of insurance to protect health care workers and facilities against medical malpractice suits is an enormous, hidden expense. The fear of these suits also causes many physicians to request or perform unnecessary and expensive tests in order to rule out improbable disorders. The AMA estimates the annual cost of superfluous laboratory work at $21 billion.[33] Both malpractice insurance and lawsuits can be reduced by legally enforceable, right to sue waiver contracts. When patients sign these agreements, they allow physicians to carry out risky but life saving procedures without fear of legal action. An intermediate step is practiced by Kaiser Permanente. As a part of the consent to medical care agreement, the patient accepts arbitration if legal action is necessary. This eliminates high attorney fees and excessive malpractice settlements. In other countries, patients who have legitimate malpractice claims receive court awarded settlements based upon computer analysis of all aspects of the medical procedure, the injury or illness and the impact on the patient. Malpractice suits could also be reduced by determining a general consensus among physicians regarding the appropriate treatment for an illness. This concept has been initiated by the use of DRG (diagnostic related group) which is a fee schedule currently used by some insurance companies to determine acceptable treatment. This would support the validity of individual physician decisions, reduce unnecessary tests and treatment and decrease the chances of malpractice suits.

Pharmaceutical Companies

Changing the types of new drugs developed by the major pharmaceutical companies would better meet the health needs of most Americans. These companies now spend large amounts of money to produce new medications which already have successful competitors in the marketplace. For instance, there are many effective drugs available for the treatment of arthritis yet companies have developed over twenty non steroidal, anti-inflammatory agents, none of which differ significantly in the relief of symptoms or production of side affects. The major reason these new drugs are developed is an attempt to capture a share of the financially lucrative market. The government could use tax incentives to direct pharmaceutical companies toward the development of new and needed medications rather than duplicates of presently successful drugs.

Patient Expectations

Successful implementation of most cost-reducing programs must be preceded by a change in the attitude of the American public regarding health care availability. Historically our system has shielded patients from the real cost. Thus we regard all types of medical treatment not as a privilege but as an unlimited right which we should receive upon demand. If we are going to cut our medical expenses, we must reduce patient expectations for expensive procedures which provide few benefits. Through education, Americans can come to the realization that health care is a limitless need which is making demands on a limited resource.

Conclusion

Finally, the current dilemma in American health care can be resolved by implementing a multitude of proven, cost-saving techniques. This includes placing the responsibility for reducing preventable disease on the shoulders of those who cause their own illness. It also involves placing realistic limits on expensive professional health care and eliminating unnecessary and inefficient practices in the medical profession. These changes can be initiated by using a variety of social and economic incentives. The resulting savings should enable us to provide adequate care to those who are currently in need.

CHAPTER EIGHT

ENVIRONMENT AND ENERGY

Future City

As the sun rises to provide life giving energy, we emerge for a day of work, education or recreation. Our theoretical town is one of many which have been created by dividing our decaying mega-cities into smaller functioning communities. Urban planners, engineers, ecologists, and business people have combined their creative talents and used our current technology to design these smaller towns around the needs of the residents. They contain the necessary housing, schools, business, industry and natural areas; all inter-connected by safe and dependable public transportation. Some of us travel to work or school infrequently because we are employed or educated primarily in our homes using computers, teleconferencing and interactive, televised educational programs. Energy consumption has been reduced in all buildings with insulation, double pane windows and energy efficient appliances. The three "R"s (reduce, reuse and recycle) are built into our new communities. In homes, business and industry unnecessary consumption is reduced and where possible, toxic materials have been replaced with harmless substitutes. Through a "swap meet" located next to the recycling and disposal center, reusable materials are returned to the community. We maintain local parks and natural areas and also reach outside of our town to nearby ecosystems to repair the environmental damage inflicted by unregulated pollution and habitat destruction. Since many of the problems in our former large, malfunctioning cities were initiated by overcrowding, each new town has a population limit. Once this has been reached, no additional building is allowed. Other people must occupy nearby towns or build communities in new locations. As a result of careful planning, cooperation and mutual effort, we have developed sustainable communities which are nice places to live. They are uncrowded, the air and water are clean and people lead busy, enjoyable and productive lives.

History

If this environmentally balanced life is our goal, how can it be achieved? Assuming that an understanding of our past will give us some direction into our future, let's turn the clock back a few thousand years. Small, hunting and gathering tribes of Native Americans worshiped and respected the land and depended upon the environment for their survival. Later, European-Americans occupied this rich land and began to exploit the natural resources. Expanding across the continent, they carried out an agricultural and industrial revolution which used or wasted most of this abundance.

As we entered modern times, space exploration gave us our first view of the entire earth. From an orbiting satellite, our home appeared to us as a relatively small planet with a limited life support system. Observations from space also revealed the massive damage resulting from human activities.

People Respond

As the public became aware of these major problems, many turned to established environmental groups for solutions. As a result, these groups grew in numbers and power and intensified their efforts. New laws were enacted in an attempt to force business, industry and even government to reduce pollution. Initially, private enterprise was dragged screaming toward changes which would produce a cleaner environment. The reason for their resistance was primarily economic. Externalizing the cost of environmental damage (letting someone else pay for it) was increasing short-term corporate profits. However, the violation of environmental laws often resulted in large fines and occasional prison sentences for top executives. These corporate leaders also began to realize that they and their families were consuming toxins and breathing pollutants along with everyone else. Out of concern for their public image, economic well being and personal health, many executives became reluctant environmentalists and compliance with regulations increased. Often investments in pollution control, waste recycling and energy conservation increased long-term income. But the continued emphasis on quick profits along with the absence of creative political alternatives such as economic incentives or third party arbitration, prevented major breakthroughs.

Earth Day 1990 arrived and as a result of the highly publicized festivities, many people decided to make environmentalism a part of their lives. New programs were initiated and many had a general feeling that we were successfully resolving our environmental dilemma. But as continued scientific study revealed the enormity of the problems, we began to realize that the solutions would require major life style changes and the expenditure of billions of dollars.

Ecocentric Lifestyle

The commitment necessary to clean up our environment and restore natural ecosystems can only be generated by a change in our basic philosophy of life. Our current anthropocentric or human centered view of the earth casts us as sculptors, carving out a world to meet our own needs and wants. With our enlarged cerebrum and opposable thumb, we have developed a technology which has enabled us to conquer nature. We assume the position of gods and look down over our subjugated earth. As the new deity, we are in control of and separate from nature. We believe our water comes from faucets rather than streams or aquifers and our food from supermarkets rather than farms. Our strained ecosystems groan under the stress exerted by hoards of humans taking all that they want as quickly as possible from a fragile planet. But natural laws are violated and eventually we pay the penalty. While thousand-year-old stands of native trees quietly succumb to clear-cutting, winter rains, unimpeded by plant cover, flood our homes and cities, destroy our freshwater fisheries and carry our precious topsoil to the floor of our oceans. In response, we attempt to patch up a few holes in our ecosystems and continue to live a declining but still acceptable lifestyle with the remaining resources of a deteriorating earth. But our children, grandchildren and the other members of the earth's future generations will have little to sustain them. We will have used or destroyed both ours and theirs.

Our new philosophy must lead to the preservation of our life support system, which includes our living ecosystems and the physical environment which supports them. We must also reduce the over consumption of our resources and the pollution of our planet. To fail to adopt an ecologically centered philosophy is to eventually perish.

An Environmental Future

We can renew our membership in the natural world, obey the ecological laws and become responsible participants in the world's ecosystems by conserving native plants and animals both for their intrinsic and economic values. We will also practice sustainable yield harvest, taking only those renewable resources which are replaced by the normal process of growth and reproduction. While conserving and regulating the use of our non renewable minerals and petroleum resources, we will search for alternatives. Finally, human-generated waste will be returned to the natural environment only in a form and amount which can be incorporated into natural cycles. Those toxins which will not recycle in nature must be rendered harmless through chemical treatment or the use of genetically engineered bacteria.

Our earth centered philosophy will have a reference point by which we can determine the extent of human-caused variation from natural systems. This baseline is wilderness; natural areas containing unmodified ecosystems. The few remaining, irreplaceable islands of wilderness will be saved for future generations. They will also be enlarged by extending their boundaries into adjacent agricultural or grazing areas which will no longer be required for commercial production. Native plants and animals can naturally extend their range into these surrounding areas. The reestablishment of wilderness will be assisted by zoos and botanical gardens which reintroduce native organisms cultured in breeding programs. People will be able to experience wilderness in order to understand and appreciate the natural world and their relationship to nature. Human access to expanding wilderness will be increased but regulated to prevent damage to the habitat and wildlife. Large sections of wilderness will be returned to indigenous people with the requirement that it be sustained to preserve their culture.

Major Environmental Problems — Deforestation

We must also come to grips with the major problems which threaten our earth. Deforestation involves not only the loss of native trees but also the life-sustaining topsoil and the natural habitat for thousands of other plants and animals. Forests are harvested for a variety of reasons: timber, fuel-wood for cooking and heating, agriculture, livestock grazing, mining, reservoir construction and urbanization. Almost without exception, we are depleting our forests by cutting them in an unsustainable manner. Even tree farming, the replanting of forests for future cutting, is far behind current harvest. We have already removed one-third of the earth's total forests. The natural reestablishment of these forests to their original composition, if it occurs at all, requires from 200 to 2,000 years. At the current rate of harvest or destruction, most of the world's natural forests, which contain fifty to ninety percent of the world's bio-diversity, will be lost in next thirty to forty years.

Not only is deforestation ecologically destructive but it is also bad economics. During its lifetime, a typical tree in a tropical forest provides almost $200,000 worth of ecological benefits including crops, erosion prevention and wild life habitat. The same tree is worth only about $600 when cut and sold for commercial use. Forests also provide other human benefits. While tropical rain forests provide twenty-five percent of the raw materials needed to produce our life-saving drugs, only one percent of the plants from these areas have been studied for their medicinal properties. Most of the world's major agricultural crops including rice, wheat and corn were developed from wild strains of these plants in tropical forests. The remaining plants are the only biological reference libraries for future medicines and crop plants. Trees also affect forest climate by providing 50-80 percent of the moisture for rainfall. In many large deforested areas, as rainfall decreases the climate becomes hot and dry and the ecosystem changes to a sparse grassland or desert.

There are many ways of preserving forests. When provided with information regarding harmful environmental practices, consumers will often boycott products. The boycott of tuna caught in dolphin killing purse seine nets forced a change in fishing methods and a resulting decrease in the destruction of dolphins. If all wood and wood products are labeled with the area of origin and method of harvest, a selective boycott will reduce unsustainable harvest. Americans can also make selective purchases of nuts, fruits and rubber which will financially support the sustainable harvest of tropical forests in poor countries, enabling the people living in these areas to rise out of poverty without destroying their environment. Over a fifty-year period, this type of sustainable harvest would generate twice the income as timber production in the same area and three times as much as cattle ranching.[132] Forests can also be preserved by terminating international funding for new roads into pristine areas. These roads bring unsustainable commercial logging operations and farmers who practice ecologically damaging agriculture. Eco-tourism is another strategy used to save forests. Biologist Daniel Janzen is restoring a tropical lowland forest in Costa Rica. He plans to involve 40,000 local people who will plant seedlings and serve as educational guides.

Desertification

Due to unsustainable agricultural practices, the formation of new deserts threatens major farming areas in the western and midwestern portions of the United States. Worldwide, threatened grasslands and scrub forests are the size of both North and South America. At the current rate, desertification will threaten the livelihood of 1.2 billion people by the year 2000.[133]

New deserts are formed in different ways: prolonged drought, over grazing, farming on thin, erodible soils, deforestation and soil compaction by cattle and machinery. The result is decreased agricultural productivity or the loss of natural vegetation which leads to soil erosion. Accelerated by overpopulation and poverty in developing countries, it ultimately results in famine and environmental refugees.

Desertification can be slowed by reducing its human causes. Since these areas have a very low carrying capacity, human populations must be reduced in the deserts of the poor countries. In the short term incentives can be used to induce people to move to other suitable, geographical regions. In the long term birth rates must be reduced. Also, cultural values can be changed through education.

Overgrazing results when goats, sheep and cattle are accumulated as symbols of wealth and prestige by desert nomads. Substituting other forms of wealth will decrease the herds to the minimum level needed to support the people and reduce their negative impact upon the land. In all areas of the world, desert agriculture can be confined to the flood plains of rivers or carried out in other areas with a minimum amount of irrigation to prevent the accumulation of salt in the soil.

Once the human activities resulting in desertification are significantly reduced, these areas can be restored to their former grassland, brush or forest habitat. This type of rehabilitation is a sound economic as well as ecological investment. The total cost of the restoration of deserts formed by humans would be about $141 billion. This is approximately five and one-half times the estimated $26 billion current annual loss in agricultural productivity from these areas. Thus, the cost of restoration could be recouped in about six years.[132]

Greenhouse Effect

Although it is a controversial issue, most knowledgeable scientists agree that the earth's average temperature is measurably increasing. The disagreement lies primarily in the current rate of change and the ultimate impact on the earth and its ecosystems. The increasing temperature is caused by an envelope of heat trapping gasses which are produced primarily as a result of human activities. These include excessive carbon dioxide, methane, CFCs and oxides of nitrogen. These gasses prevent heat at the surface of the earth from making its normal escape into the atmosphere. Projections for many regions include a decrease in rainfall and a reduction in agricultural production. Other areas are predicted to experience an increase in precipitation however, due to poor soils, many of these regions will not produce more food. Around the world, native plants and animals are now trapped in the small island-like ecosystems of national parks and remaining wilderness areas. Subjected to climate change and surrounded by farmlands or urban areas, they will not have the necessary time or the normal avenues for dispersal to other suitable habitats and many will succumb.

Global warming could also result in an expansion of the world's oceans and an acceleration in the melting rate of the polar ice caps. Collectively this would result in an elevation in the level of the oceans. Since most of the major cities of the world exist at or near sea level, this rise, accompanied by winter storm waves, could eventually result in major damage to most of the world's population centers along with coastal harbors and wetlands.

Because there are some studies which indicate that the results of global warming could be of little consequence, many oppose action on this problem. But to debate the possible environmental results is to miss the point. Even if the greenhouse effect were a myth, all of the proposed solutions should be implemented for other verifiable economic reason (see the energy section of this chapter). This includes the termination of the wasteful burning of both our limited fossil fuels and our forests and a transition to other energy sources.

The Ozone Layer

CFC gasses not only contribute to the greenhouse effect but are also destroying our protective layer of atmospheric ozone. The resulting increased human exposure to ultra violet light is producing a significantly higher incidence of human melanoma skin cancer. The protection of the ozone layer must begin with an immediate, worldwide ban on the use of CFCs in foam plastic production, aerosol sprays and air conditioning units. Until an environmentally safe substitute is found, we can replace CFCs with currently available alternatives such as HFCs (hydro fluorocarbons) and HCFCs (hydro chlorofluorocarbons). These chemicals have ozone depleting potentials of only two to ten percent of CFCs.

Toxic Waste

One of our most important and least understood environmental problems is toxic waste. Chemical and metal factories along with the petroleum refining industries produce about ninety-three percent of the 500 million tons of federally defined hazardous waste generated each year. The GAO (Government Accounting Office) estimates that there are between 103,000 and 425,000 different locations in the U.S. which contain potentially hazardous wastes. In addition there are 17,000 sites on U.S. military bases and nuclear weapons facilities. By 1991 the EPA had cleaned up only sixty-four of these sites at an average cost of twenty-six million dollars each. The total cleanup cost is estimated at $500 billion; however, the real cost could be far greater because only ten percent of our commercial chemicals have been thoroughly examined for toxicity and only two percent have been adequately tested to determine if they cause cancer, birth defects or genetic mutations. For the most part we still do not know the type, quantity, or synergistic effects (results of the combination of chemicals) of the toxins we breath, eat or drink. This is because the scientific risk-benefit analysis of a new chemical is expensive, time consuming and often produces controversial results. To complicate matters further, disease, disorders or death from exposure to toxic chemicals are usually veiled because they result from long term, low level exposure. The symptoms are often subclinical, chronic and could be caused by exposure to several different chemicals. We see occasional "epidemics" of disease in toxic work places or within groups of people living near toxic dump sites however establishing a causative relationship between the toxin and specific human disorder is often impossible. We do have valid data on the effects of some of these chemicals. For example, eighty-eight percent of American children under six years of age have lead levels in their blood which could retard their development.[132]

There are a variety of ineffective toxic waste disposal methods currently used in the U.S. Most of this waste is "eliminated" by deep well injection with no guarantee that the poisons will not move into shallow aquifers which supply drinking water. Surface evaporation ponds are another common method of "disposal". According to the EPA, ninety percent of our toxic waste may either threaten ground water supplies or release volatile organic solvents into the atmosphere. Approximately five percent of the toxins are buried underground. According to the Office of Technology Assessment, all of the containers in these landfills will eventually leak and their contents will be able to move into the ground water. Only five percent of the hazardous waste in America is detoxified, recycled or reused.

How can we safely and effectively deal with the toxic byproducts of our industrialized society? The least expensive method is to eliminate the chemical by modifying industrial processes. Since 1975 the 3M Company has reduced its hazardous waste production by sixty-six percent and as a result, has saved over $500 million. This was accomplished by redesigning equipment and manufacturing processes which allows for the use of safer raw materials. Other methods include detoxifying by dilution or neutralization and decomposition using natural or bio-engineered bacteria. Between fifteen and thirty percent of the industrial toxins currently in use could be reused or recycled. The EPA estimates that sixty percent of all U.S. hazardous waste could be safely incinerated. Public acceptance of this process will require extensive citizen education, large investments in equipment and proper treatment and disposal of the remaining toxic ash.

The control of toxins can be financed in a variety of ways. Incentives include tax breaks for the implementation of new technologies leading to the elimination of these chemicals while disincentives require a tax on each unit of waste generated. Legislation and economic incentives would also result in the development of new industries to remove toxins from the soil and water.

Energy

In many ways our environmental problems are related to our energy policies. These complex rules and laws are the result of compromises between powerful pressure groups with divergent points of view. Business, industry, conservation organizations and consumers often promote their own interests at the expense of functional solutions. The result is an American energy policy which does not work.

Petroleum

The life blood of America and the other industrialized societies of the world is petroleum. Although there is controversy regarding both the amount and accessibility of the earth's remaining reserves, experts realize that the supply is both physically and economically limited. Unfortunately, we are driven by simple market demand to consume the earth's remaining oil in a rapid and wasteful manner.

This gives rise to many environmental problems. As we burn gasoline, we are increasing the greenhouse effect by adding excessive carbon dioxide to our atmosphere. The high cost of petroleum also has a negative impact on our nation's economy. Almost half of our oil is imported and this contributes extensively to our foreign debt. A large portion of our oil comes from the Middle East. If we assume that the numerous American military incursions in the Persian Gulf area are carried out primarily to ensure the continuous flow of oil, the real cost of Middle East petroleum is about $500 per barrel.[121] We pay this enormous price for large quantities of oil as a result of the tremendous political power of the automobile and petroleum industries. These companies make a greater profit per unit on expensive, low milage cars and American consumers continue to buy these automobiles due to aggressive advertising and the artificially low cost of gasoline at the pump.

Automobiles have been developed which meet performance, safety and emission standards comparable to our present vehicles and also offer fuel efficiency in excess of 100 miles per gallon. If government benefits for petroleum producers are reduced, the true cost would pass from the general taxpayer to the consumer. Accompanied by the mass production of fuel efficient automobiles, the development of rapid transit and car and van pools, we would significantly reduce consumption. In order to encourage efficiency and reduced dependence on foreign oil, Western European countries have reduced or eliminated petroleum tax breaks and subsidies. They have also added a sales tax to gasoline and developed extensive and well run rapid transit systems.

Nuclear Energy

The nuclear power industry represents itself as a clean, safe, inexpensive and practically inexhaustible energy source for the future. Three Mile Island and Chernobyl leave many unconvinced. However, aside from their few, spectacular failures, nuclear energy should be phased out for a far more practical and demonstrable reason. It is simply too expensive. In order to determine the true and total cost of nuclear energy, we must include the cleverly hidden, taxpayer-funded government subsidies. Other enormous expenses include the location of a safe and suitable site for the power plant and compliance with the complex construction requirements needed to insure the present and future safety of the facility. One of the greatest costs of nuclear energy is just beginning to emerge: the decommissioning and dismantling of nuclear power plants when they reach the end of their approximately thirty year life span. Previously it was hoped that future technological breakthroughs would enable us to accomplish this cleanup safely and inexpensively, however, this new technology has not emerge. In 1986 none of the non-functioning plants had been decommissioned or dismantled and by 2010, sixty-seven large, commercial American power plants are scheduled to close. The future cost of cleaning up and removing these plants is estimated at between fifty million and three billion dollars per plant.[151] This cleanup also requires the reprocessing of used nuclear fuel rods which are currently stored on site. Presently there are only two functioning reprocessing plants in the world, one in England and the other in France.

Conservation

Since petroleum and nuclear energy have numerous, major disadvantage, we must look for another future source of affordable energy. Oddly enough, all energy experts agree that the least expensive potential source of "new" energy is conservation. By using less energy to accomplish the same amount of work, the cost is decreased. This new source will produce no harmful waste, strengthen our national economy and improve our international balance of trade. Lets consider some examples. By adding variable speed drives and other available energy efficient devices to electric motors in industry, we could reduce our energy usage by an amount equal to the energy produced by all of the present U.S. nuclear power plants. If we added fuel efficiency devices costing up to $330 to each American car, by the year 2000 we would increase the average milage to between fifty-one and seventy-eight miles per gallon and eliminate the need to import any foreign oil.[121] Finally, by using currently available, cost-effective technology and reducing energy waste in U.S. buildings, factories and vehicles, we could reduce our national energy consumption by forty-three percent. Even with our present meager efforts to promote increased efficiency, we have managed to cut our national energy bill by 160 billion dollars annually. If we invest fifty billion dollars per year in energy efficiency, we can benefit our country in many ways. This will stimulate the economy, decrease the cost of producing goods and services, make the U.S. more competitive and save 250 billion dollars per year.[135] The immediate implementation of currently available energy efficiency and waste prevention techniques, coupled with a long-term transition to perpetual and renewable energy sources such has as solar, wind, hydroelectric and biomass, would enable America to meet its total energy needs by 2030.

At the same time we should initiate a policy which will initially be opposed by most business people and economists: the transfer of this new technology directly to the poor, developing countries. Why should America give away its expensive and hard-won technology? Because this will allow these countries to bypass the expensive polluting coal and oil stage of energy usage. As they industrialize, they will be able to move directly to conservation and perpetual and renewable energy sources. This will allow them to expand their economies tenfold with no increase in energy use. This proposal offers numerous benefits for America; reduced poverty-driven immigration to our country, increased foreign buying power to purchase U.S. products, a potential for political and economic stability and a reduced risk of local wars.

Human Population

Ultimately the solution to all of our environmental problems rests upon our ability to implement a massive reduction in human birth rates. Many Americans believe that increasing populations are only a problem in the developing countries. However, there are two human population explosions. The first is the increase in the number of poor people in Africa, Latin America and many Asian countries. The second is subtle, less obvious but very important. It is "consumption over population": the excessive individual consumption of resources characterized by the citizens in the developed countries of Europe, Asia and North America.[63]

The people of earth share one planet, one home. There are no other options, none in outer space or on the floor of the ocean. The solutions to all of our environmental and energy problems are at hand. If we choose to do so, we can resolve our environmental dilemma and also build the communities described at the beginning of this chapter.

CHAPTER NINE

AGRICULTURE

Introduction

On most spring days John Vogelsburg, an elderly farmer in bib overalls, can be seen driving a 1940 vintage tractor on his 860-acre farm near Home, Kansas. John's family has farmed this same land for over 100 years. During this entire period of time, no chemical fertilizers, pesticides or herbicides have been used on the crops or the land. According to John these chemicals are expensive, unnecessary and harmful. In order to conserve the topsoil, he practices crop rotation and diversification by planting corn, soybeans, wheat and oats in fifteen acre strips. He keeps half of his farm in pasture to feed cattle and prevent erosion. To maintain soil fertility, John plants legumes which naturally add nitrogen to the soil. He eliminates weeds with a "go dig", which plows them under the ground while the crop plants are still small. Harmful insects are reduced by practicing biological control. Rather than trying to kill all of these pests, he reduces their populations to economically acceptable levels by maintaining natural predatory insects. But what about the bottom line—does John Vogelsburg make any money? He does make a profit because his crops are superior in quality and quantity to those grown on surrounding farms which use chemicals and environmentally harmful farming practices.[128]

John has a unique philosophy regarding his farm; it is called a land ethic. He views himself as a steward of the land. John believes that he has been given a sacred trust, the responsibility of using and caring for a farm which will provide food for his family and others throughout our nation and the world. Eventually this land will be passed on to the next generation to be used and cherished in the same way.

Modern Farming

Unfortunately this description resembles few of today's American farms. Most small farms have disappeared and the communities which they supported are withering away as stores, schools and churches board up their doors and windows. There are many reasons for this decline. Farming is a difficult life and everyone must work hard and share the responsibility for success or failure. Many young people have moved to the cities where they have found a less rigorous life with easier work at higher pay.

However, the major cause of the loss of family farms is the current economic policies of our government which favor the large corporate farms of agribusiness. These enormous factory farms have been painted as progress: fewer farmers producing more food. But modern agribusiness is not saving American agriculture, it is destroying it. The goals of most giant corporations are the same; maximize short-term profits for the company and the stockholders. But in the long run, agribusiness is not economically sustainable because it excludes the present and future environmental costs in its corporate spreadsheets. These enormous farms have sacrificed topsoil and water quality for profits. Throughout the Midwest, forty-seven percent of the cropland is inadequately protected from erosion. According to a USDA study in 1982, the average loss of topsoil was 8.1 tons per acre/year while replenishment varied from 1-5 tons per acre/year. Pesticides and the nitrates and phosphates in chemical fertilizers percolate into the aquifers and pollute the ground water. Tests in Iowa reveal that half of the wells are contaminated with pesticides and medical studies indicate that many local people have an excessive accumulation of these chemical residues in their bodies. Underground aquifers are pumped for irrigation faster than they can be recharged by rainfall. Much of the Ogallala aquifer, which underlies seven central states including Nebraska, Kansas and Texas, will be depleted and unusable by 2020. The amount of irrigated farmland is already decreasing in five of these seven states due to the high cost of pumping water from depths of as great as 6,000 feet.[132]

History

In order to understand how we created our current agricultural dilemma, we must look back into the history of our country. In 1837 John Deere invented the steel plow. Perhaps more than anything else, this piece of technology enabled large numbers of European Americans to pour out onto the great plains, purchase inexpensive land and cultivate crops. The westward movement was provided with what seemed to be an endless supply of rich, productive land which was used and misused as the pioneers spread across America. The new farmers discovered that agriculture, by its very nature, was complex and unstable. Crop productivity varied with weather and pests, and profits depended upon the unpredictable supply and demand of the marketplace. In an attempt to make farming economically reliable for both farmers and consumers, the federal government gradually moved in and began to regulate agriculture. This was the beginning of one of the most complex and expensive quagmires ever devised by our government. In the 1930s, our national farm policy provided minimum price guarantees for crops. There were also attempts to limit crop production in order to keep market prices above government support levels. As the years went by, federal programs were enlarged and expanded to include even more subsidies. Tariffs were used to reduce the importation of inexpensive foreign crops. The government also provided agricultural loans to grow some crops and payments to farmers to prevent the planting of others.

Following World War II, farmers continued to have difficulty selling excessive crops created by taxpayer supported subsidies. Then we found a universally acceptable market. We would feed the hungry people of the world. Excess American crops were either sold at very low prices or given to the people in poor countries. Although feeding the poor with our abundance appeared to be a good idea, it often financially undercut or destroyed the agricultural systems of these countries. Cheap American crops also supported rapidly growing human populations as people became dependent upon a temporary source of inexpensive and abundant food. We were unknowingly setting the stage for future famine in many of these countries.

Later, as international trade developed between the wealthier countries, American farming expanded to meet the demands of the apparently endless world export market. Small, "economically inefficient" farms were gradually purchased by large land owners who also assumed the accompanying government subsidies. As more government money flowed into these farms, industry quickly picked up the scent. Larger farms created a market for more chemicals and massive equipment. Following the money trail, the petrochemical corporations shifted to chemical fertilizers, pesticides and fuel for farm equipment. These farms also required enormous and expensive plows and combines, and the equipment producers fell in line to secure their share of the government loot.

The use of this massive, motorized equipment also necessitated a change in farming practices. Huge tractors and plows were more efficient when driven for long distances in a straight line. Obstructions such as trees, hedges and wetlands which protected topsoil and provided habitat for wildlife fell before the mechanized onslaught. Contour plowing of elevated areas to prevent topsoil erosion became economically inefficient and was abandoned. Other traditional practices were also changed. Plowing the fields in the fall rather than in the spring permitted earlier planting of crops and resulted in increased profits however it also exposed the bare soil to winter rains and the resulting erosion.

Agricultural Politics

The economic success of agriculture depended upon its political strength. Initially this economic giant had political feet of clay. Not only were American taxpayers unknowingly supporting both the expensive over-production of crops and the destruction of farmlands but they were doing so to assist a relatively small number of people. Agriculture wisely compensated for its lack of constituents by becoming a well organized and politically active group which included farmers, equipment and chemical producers, and farm community business people. They tithed a significant portion of their government subsidies back into the campaign funds of both Democratic and Republican candidates and became a political force second to none. Their power extended beyond farming. Politicians were eager to use the united farm block as a swing vote on other important national issues.

With its enormous political power, the farm lobby directed the complex activities of the U.S. Department of Agriculture and this agency eventually became an organizational nightmare. It manipulated interlocking prices for commodities and generated complex rules and regulations which were administered by a hugh bureaucracy. The failure of the USDA to adequately regulate agriculture was well illustrated in the 1950s when skilled, hard-working farmers produced enormous yields and a large crop surplus resulted. In response to this over production, and at the direction of the farm lobby, Congress formed the Soil Bank which paid farmers to set aside some of their farmland for conservation rather than crop production. Like any free market entrepreneur, most farmers placed their poorest soil in the "bank" and used their government funds to buy better seed and fertilizer to increase productivity on their remaining land. This resulted in increased over-production, larger surpluses and ultimately decreased crop prices and farm income.[185]

Agribusiness

As time passed, large farms continued to absorb those which were smaller. The final and almost inaudible death knell for most family farmers was sounded in the early 1970's. This began, strangely enough, with a period of agricultural prosperity. When failing Russian agriculture and world wide droughts absorbed the stored surplus crops of American farmers, Secretary of Agriculture Butz told American farmers to "plant fence row to fence row and feed the world".[185] Production on traditional farms increased however the major growth resulted from the entrance and expansion of large corporations and foreign investors. Agribusiness finally became the dominant force in American agriculture. In an attempt to compete with this profitable giant, many small farmers went into debt to purchase more land and farming equipment. Then the cost of farming skyrocketed when the oil crisis of 1973 increased the price of fuel along with petroleum based fertilizers and pesticides. Traditional conservation farming practices were cast aside in a desperate attempt to maximize profits. In response to the demands for more irrigation water, federally sponsored water projects pumped aquifers faster than they could be recharged.

In the early 1980s, for a variety of reasons, the agricultural roller coaster suddenly turned downward. American exports declined as a result of both an overvalued dollar and President Carter's grain boycott against Russia in response to the invasion of Afghanistan. At the same time, American agriculture faced fierce competition in the world market. Foreign grain production increased and despite American subsidies, crops from other countries were cheaper than our own. Surplus grain accumulated in America, commodity prices continued to fall and family farmers with excessive debt could not make their large mortgage payments. More families began to lose their farms and the number of foreclosures increased to the highest level since the great depression. Many who had provided food for America for generations lost their farms, their homes and their way of life and they were often driven into poverty and city slums. For many good, hard-working Americans a noble way of life was gone.

While family farms reverted to the banks, agribusiness corporations, with their large financial reserves, survived the downturn. They purchased these farms and acquired the accompanying subsidies which provided them with even more economic power. Through increased campaign contributions, they expanded their political base and were in turn financially rewarded with increased subsidies by grateful politicians. Government supported agricultural income rose from seven billion dollars in 1980 to thirty-one billion in 1987. Between 1986 and 1989 taxpayers were shelling out an average of $600,000 in government subsidies for each American farmer. Because subsidies were based primarily on production, eighty percent of this money was paid to wealthy, large land holders and corporations rather than to the small family farmers for whom it was originally intended.[37] Today, the large national and multinational corporations are squeezing the last remaining dollars out of the depleted life support system of this country. Without major changes, our farmlands will soon consist of thin, contaminated topsoil and polluted and near empty aquifers. Eventually, agribusiness will respond to declining income by either selling or abandoning our farmlands and moving on to more profitable investments. The once proud bread basket of America will lay in economic and environmental ruin.

The Future—Reestablishing Family Farms

Despite our current situation, there is hope for American farming. The prototype for a new American agriculture can be found in the few remaining family farms which still practice stewardship of the land and sustainable crop production. These farmers struggle on for a variety of reasons. For many it is the only life they have ever known. Its benefits cannot be measured exclusively in leisure time or dollars. They value other qualities; the freedom of an individual business owner, clean air and open space, soil to plant and crops to harvest, and the security of a strong, supportive family which is the social and economic foundation of their rural community. These farmers, the Vogelsburgs and others like them, represent the hope for the future of American agriculture.

The resurrection must begin with a change in the economics of farming. Since subsidies and other economic policies resulted in the destruction of most family farms, new and different government programs must be established to initiate their restoration. The economic foundation for a new American agriculture can be a single subsidy; a government price guarantee paid only for crops grown on family farms and small partnerships. To insure that participating farmers receive a fair income for their crops, the price support will be established annually by a governmental agency. If the price on the market is lower, the government can pay the difference in cash. If the market price is higher, the farmer will keep the profit and receive nothing from the government. It will be necessary to prevent over production with a cap on the number of subsidized acres. For example, subsidies for each family can be provided for approximately 320 acres in the corn belt and 640 acres in wheat growing areas. Additional acres which are owned and farmed will not be eligible for this economic support.[185]

In order to qualify for subsidies, family farmers must agree to practice sustainable agriculture. This will include restoration of the depleted topsoil with nitrogen producing cover crops, the addition of animal manure and unused crop plant parts. A new water management strategy can insure a continuous, dependable supply of uncontaminated ground and surface water. This will include drip irrigation and crop selection based upon water availability. Sustainability incudes a massive reduction in the use of chemical pesticides, accomplished with the use of IPM (Integrated Pest Management). This ecological technique reduces "bad bug" populations to economically harmless levels. It relies upon a variety of methods including the use of beneficial insects to prey upon those which are harmful, chemical attractants in baited traps and the introduction of sterile males to displace those which are fertile. IPM uses chemical pesticides only when other techniques fail. Other insect control methods include habitat manipulation such as crop rotation and altering crop planting times. Wildlife habitat restoration is another aspect of sustainable agriculture. Ponds will be reestablished and stream banks planted with native vegetation. The increased number of birds, coyotes and other natural predators will reduce insects, rabbits and other organisms which feed on crop plants. It is also necessary to replace monoculture, the endless miles of genetically identical crops which require excessive amounts of water, pesticides and fertilizers, with a variety of productive plants which have the genetic diversity necessary to provide natural resistance to drought, disease and pests.

Large farms owned by agribusiness or under foreign ownership will no longer receive subsidies. As a result, their value will decrease and the land will become available to potential new family farmers. How would this change affect our country? Many Americans will have access to a new and different lifestyle. Urban dwellers who are tired of congestion, crime and pollution can join a second historical migration to the new American agricultural frontier. New family farmers will be assisted in many ways. Grassroots groups such as Landlink now help young families in securing a farm home. These families are "linked" with older farmers who wish to pass their farm onto the next generation, but whose children have chosen not to go into farming. The organization arranges loans, long term payments and sweat equity (payment by work rather than money) as part of the farm loan. Low interest government loans and "rent with option to buy" programs can also provide the needed financial assistance for other new farmers. Educational programs describing the techniques of sustainable farming will be developed and presented in local adult schools and on public television. Experienced family farmers and agricultural experts united with new farm families will pass on the necessary skills, traditions and culture. As these new farms become the centerpiece of American agriculture, other societal institutions can move to their support. Family farming methods will improve as educational and research programs in agricultural colleges and universities move from an agribusiness orientation to the support of sustainable farming.

These land stewards will form new, efficient economic systems; local cooperative groups will develop decentralized marketing systems to bypass the current layers of processors, middlemen and lengthy distribution which absorb much of the agricultural profits. Consumers will have greater access to less expensive food which is fresh, grown locally and uncontaminated. The Federal Crop Grading standards currently eliminate much of the nutritious food from the marketplace due to the cosmetic appearance of the crop. Consumers will learn that the harmless spots or blemishes on plants are a result of ecologically sound methods of pest control which reduce or eliminate the need for chemical pesticides. They will demand grading based upon nutritional value and pesticide residues and this will result in acceptance of these safer, higher quality foods.[185] Farmers will also reduce costs by decreasing their dependence on expensive foreign oil. They can move away from petroleum based fertilizers and pesticides and also use smaller mechanical equipment which requires less fuel.

Farm Products, Health and Environment

The products of family farms will gradually change as consumers are educated regarding the harmful health and environmental effects of raising and consuming large quantities of cattle and other farm animals. Many of these products are high in cholesterol and saturated fats, a major dietary contributor to the number one killer in our society: cardiovascular disease. Because animals are higher in the food chain, they also concentrate pesticides in their meat and milk and pass these contaminants on to consumers. The production of large numbers of farm animals is also responsible for the use of enormous quantities of water, both directly through animal consumption and indirectly to irrigate the crops which are raised for animal feed.

Animals raised for human food consume eighty percent of our crop plants. This includes one-half of the grain produced in this country.

If Americans reduced their intake of animal products by only thirty percent, we could reduce the land used for current agricultural products by seventy-five percent.[159] This land would have many beneficial uses. Some could be placed in a soil bank and preserved for future agricultural needs. Since forests previously occupied eighty-five percent of our eastern agricultural land, these areas could also be used for silviculture or "tree agriculture". This would enable us to meet our present and future timber needs without destroying our few remaining old growth forests. Much of this land could also be restored to the original ecosystems and then added to our diminishing recreational and wilderness areas.[132]

Imports and Exports

As needed, government subsidies could be altered to support the production of surplus crops for local storage or export. Our agricultural exports can be selectively used to increase farm income and also assist in developing a balance of trade with other countries. However these exports need to be regulated by a broad foreign policy which is designed to assist sustainable agricultural systems in poor developing countries. (See Chapter Ten). Many of our current agricultural exports will gradually decrease because the subsidized cost of our crops is greater than the cost of food which is grown in other countries.

Conclusion

In the future, successful American agriculture will be based upon small family farms which, supported by a land ethic, will combine historically successful techniques with modern, sustainable farming methods. With continuing education and minimal government support, they will provide the American people with safe nutritious food and fiber, indirectly assist in the development of subsistence agriculture in the poor countries and maintain a viable export/import market.

CHAPTER TEN

DEVELOPING COUNTRIES

Introduction

The developing countries of Asia, Africa and Latin America currently contain 4.1 billion people. This represents seventy-seven percent of the world's population. Nine out of ten babies are born in these regions and one million people are added to the population every four and one-half days. For most the quality of life is poor. They are often without adequate food, water, shelter, employment or medical care. As a result, sixty thousand humans die prematurely each day. Half of these are children under five years of age and most succumb to preventable disorders such as malnutrition or diarrhea.[133]

Because of its proximity, people from the United States often vacation in the luxury hotels or beach resorts of Latin America. However, they seldom venture into the teeming city slums or poor rural areas to see the rapidly ticking human time bomb. Here, forty percent of the families live in poverty and twenty percent are so destitute that they cannot afford to purchase food to maintain an adequate diet.[70]

Seated in our living room at home, we occasionally we catch a glimpse of this poverty on the evening news. Because the problems faced by these people appear to be unsolvable, we are often overwhelmed by "compassion fatigue" and relieved when our attention is quickly diverted to the next major news item.

History of Latin America

How did so many Latin Americans become so poor? We can only understand the current poverty by looking at the history of this region. During the period of exploration and conquest, Europeans overwhelmed the native cultures of this region and forced the people to plunder their own natural resources; first to provide gold, silver and precious stones and later timber, rubber and petroleum to fuel the industrial revolution in the developed world. Later, land and power were assumed by a small group of local elite. Many of these new leaders were careful understudies of former colonial governments who ruled by brutally suppressing any who opposed their regime. In an attempt to maintain power over the growing number of poor people, the local elite often formed coalitions with the police, the military or the hierarchy of the Catholic Church. These unstable alliances periodically formed and then collapsed and the resulting political instability gave rise to a vicious cycle. First, governments were elected by promising the people large, expensive social programs which, when instituted, led to massive inflation. The cycle continued and inflation resulted in instability and unrest which was usually followed by a military takeover. This resulted in further suppression of the people. Eventually the military allowed elections and the cycle began again. Recently some political leaders have attempted to reverse this pattern with austerity measures to bring inflation under control; however, these policies have created even greater hardship and unrest among the poor.

Current Situation

For the most part political systems are infiltrated with massive corruption and well lubricated with bribes and payoffs. This process is often perpetuated with the support of American foreign policy which seeks to insure the stability necessary to maintain profitable American and multinational businesses at the expense of justice for a majority of the people. Our government also rewards the elite in power with foreign aid. The American people believe these funds are used to help the poor; however, most of the money is either stolen, wasted or expended to purchase weapons to suppress the people.

Fueling the political and economic problems, the increasing population of poor people outraces the GDP. Birth rates remain high while death rates decline due to imported health care and high technology agriculture. Initially we were told the population problem would be solved by the Green Revolution: the introduction of new, genetically superior and productive crop plants. Food production did increase in many areas however poor farmers were often unable to purchase the expensive seed, fertilizer, pesticides and farm equipment needed to grow these new "miracle" plants. Increasing poverty caused farmers to fall back to traditional, low yield but locally dependable crops as they were driven onto marginal lands with steep slopes, poor soil and low productivity.[132]

Today poor farmers are also hampered by artificially low food prices established by the government. This is an attempt to prevent hunger and the resulting unrest among the millions of urban poor gathered in the large cities. The economics of local food production are further disrupted when free or inexpensive surplus American grain is periodically "dumped" in the country. Ironically, while rural farmers and urban slum dwellers suffer from malnutrition or starvation, wealthy landowners and international agribusiness often maintain a lucrative export business with plantation "cash" crops such as coffee and bananas. "Starving countries" often quietly export more food than they import.

Massive poverty in Latin America and the other poor countries of the world is also maintained by the large debt owed to the governments and banks of the developed countries. The cumulative foreign debt of all of the developing countries is $1.2 trillion. Meeting the scheduled repayments is impossible. In an attempt to service this debt, they must make an annual interest payment of $178 billion. This is a staggering forty-four percent of their GDP.[133] These interest payments can be made only by the excessive harvest and sale of natural resources, including timber, petroleum and iron ore. National or multinational corporations often profit from this over exploitation of resources through projects which are financed by two groups which were originally designed to assist the poor people of the developing countries, the World Bank and the International Monetary Fund. Under current conditions the developing countries will never be able to pay off their debt. As they struggle to meet the interest payments, the people will remain bonded servants to the developed countries.

Finally, the ability of developing countries to generate income has declined. Since 1980, due to decreased demand or over-production, the world market price for many of their export commodities has decreased. This includes coffee, tea and mineral resources such as copper. Trade barriers erected by developed countries have further reduced the ability of poor countries to export some of their products and they have lost $50 to $100 billion annually in anticipated income.

The Struggle to Survive

Despite these enormous problems, poor people continue the struggle to maintain and improve their quality of life. But the wealthy elite usually resist attempts to change the status quo. At times the poor respond with nonviolent protest such as strikes or blockades. Others occupy large farms and ranches and are often violently dispersed by private armies or government soldiers.

Escape

Returning to Latin America, tens of millions of poor people are left with only two basic choices. They can either move to their own large cities and live a short, poverty-stricken life or, in hopes of attaining a better future, they can migrate to the United States. For those who choose the shorter trip, Mexico City serves as an example of the new future faced by these migrants. In search of a better life, fifteen hundred peasants from rural areas arrive each day. They build illegal dwellings of plastic and cardboard on marginal lands which are subject to landslides, floods and water pollution. Due either to lack of funds or out of fear they will encourage more squatters, the city government often refuses to provide water or sanitation for these slums. Tons of human waste and garbage pile up in gutters and vacant lots, attracting hordes of rats and flies. Human health also declines due to severe air pollution which is equivalent to smoking two packs of cigarettes each day from birth.[132] Mexico City mirrors other Latin American megacities. Ringed and infiltrated with slums and shanty towns which double in size every five years, crime and disease are common. These conditions also support and sustain guerilla insurgencies. The military, and in many cases right wing death

squads, respond with even greater violence against any actual or sus-
pected anti government groups or individuals.[5]

Massive Immigration

Many poor people are choosing the second option and are moving north. Currently the U.S. Border Patrol estimates that between
two and three million people illegally enter the United States from
Latin America and the Caribbean countries each year.[112] Since most
experts anticipate no significant improvement in Latin America, a
frightening possible scenario emerges. The future may unfold as follows: Because of the growing poverty and high birth rates, the number of illegal immigrants increases dramatically. Eventually tens of
millions of those who are physically able to migrate begin to move
north. They travel by bus, train, boat or on foot from Mexico and
Central and South America. It is one of the largest migrations in
human history and thousands of people, primarily women and children die in route. Some are killed by border bandits, while others die
of dehydration or starvation in the great deserts of Mexico and the
American Southwest. Smugglers transport refugees by sea to remote
beaches along the U.S. coast and many of these "boat people" drown
when their boats sink in storms. In an attempt to repel the growing
number of refugees, the military uses expensive and sophisticated
electronic detection equipment along our entire southern border. Despite these efforts, tens of millions enter the United States. Many
occupy enormous slums in and around our large southwestern cities
including Phoenix, San Diego and Los Angeles while others migrate
to central or northern states seeking work. Our social services are
overwhelmed and the shanty towns which form in and around major
U.S. cities begin to resemble the massive slums of Mexico City. An
impossible futuristic story? Only time will tell, however current conditions leave room for few, if any, alternatives.

American Attitudes

What can we do, if anything, to prevent the suffering of people
in the developing world and the eventual onslaught of Latin American immigrants into this country? When asked this question, Americans respond in a variety of ways. Some are unconcerned and simply
ignore the problem. Many want all of the illegals hauled south across

the border. Others offer simplistic solutions: poor people should stay in their own country, practice contraception, grow their own food or get a job. Out of compassion for starving children or dying ecosystems, many make a small, conscience-appeasing donation to a benevolent organization.

Buried beneath this current ambivalence and confusion, there is an American history and tradition of helping the less fortunate of the world to help themselves. We have done this because we believe that it is the moral and ethical thing to do. We feel proud of ourselves and our country when we see starving children fed and sick people cared for as a result of our generosity. This attitude has not disappeared. It has only been submerged below the other major problems we face in our country.

Solutions—Small Loans

With a relatively small investment, America can help turn the developing world around and allow the people of these countries to provide themselves with a decent standard of living. If we choose to address these problems, we must begin by dealing with poverty. The solution begins with the experts, those who are poor. These people need a small loan to start a business or a farm in order to support themselves and their families and in turn establish an economic base for their country. One successful example is the Grameen or "village" bank of Bangladesh; India's poor, neighboring country. It makes an average loan of $67 and boasts a repayment rate of ninety-eight percent. The banks 1.2 million borrowers are primarily women who use the capital to grow crops or start a small business. The resulting economic prosperity has brought improved education and health care and raised the status of women.[93]

Because most people in developing countries are rural farmers, assistance should begin here. When small, long term, low interest loans are made to poor farmers, they can lease or purchase land and develop small scale, sustainable farms and cooperative distribution systems to market their crops. These agricultural systems are locally organized, inexpensive and ultimately self-sufficient. The crop plants are those which are genetically adapted to and historically successful in local agriculture. Irrigation methods involve simple systems and animal manures are used to fertilize crops. Labor is derived from humans or draft animals.

New Economic Systems

Once successful farms have been established and the people have an adequate and dependable food supply, they will begin to move out of poverty. This will be accomplished by forming a free market system and using the profits to rebuild their families and communities. Development will include housing, water supplies, sanitation, education, businesses, health care and family planning services. A gradual removal of government price controls on food can make farming financially attractive to the urban poor and, with government incentives, many will return to rural agriculture. Others who remain in the towns and cities will be able to start small businesses. This in turn will lead to political and economic stability which can attract large, national and international corporations.

Foreign Policy

To assist in the development of these programs, American foreign policy can be used to exert political and economic pressure on the entrenched power structure of foreign governments. These political leaders can be induced to initiate land reform programs which require the owners of enormous farms to sell portions of their land to the poor at a fair price. They can be motivated by selective sanctions on the importation of luxury cash crops. Foreign aid, government loans and favorable trade relations will also be contingent upon these reforms. To prevent foreign government officials from spending or stealing the American aid designated to help needy people, these projects can be administered by responsible, accountable groups of local citizens, agencies of the American government or reputable, private international development organizations.

Trade

Assuming the previously described reforms occur, we also need to open more of our markets to the agricultural products of these poor countries. This will increase their income and in turn enable them to purchase more of our products. The developing world is a major potential market for American exports. From a purely self-serving, economic standpoint, if poor people in developing countries have no money to purchase our products, then our economy suffers.

Debt

The economic systems of developing countries will only be able to function normally when their foreign debt has been significantly reduced. This can be accomplished in several ways; debt forgiveness in exchange for the establishment of national parks (debt for nature swaps), discounting the loans (selling them for less than their original value) or "debt for development" swaps in which debtor countries repay loans in their own currency which is in turn "loaned" back to the country for environmentally sustainable development projects. Although all of these proposals are helpful, in order to provide significant debt relief, the banks of the developed countries must either significantly write down (reduce), write off (forgive) or declare a moratorium on debt repayment by poor countries. A moratorium, such as the one employed after World War II to assist the reconstruction of Japan and Germany, would enable poor countries to first rebuild their economies and then repay their debt.

Human Population

Unless human population growth is significantly reduced, the other problems in developing countries cannot be resolved. Lowering birth rates involves more than providing contraceptives. Historically, we have seen births decrease when cultural, religious and traditional attitudes change. Women have fewer children when they have access to education, employment, money and power over their own lives. Maternal and infant health care and a variety of contraceptive options also decrease birth rates. Inexpensive, convenient and effective contraceptives are now available including new IUD's and female hormones in the form of pills, injections or skin implants. Births also decline in a culture which provides care for the elderly and thus reduces the need for "social security sons."

Many of these cultural, religious and traditional changes have been occurring and by 1990, two-thirds of the women in developing countries wanted to limit the size of their families. If we increased the annual world expenditure for contraception from the current $3.2 billion to eight billion dollars, we could meet the contraceptive needs of all of the people in poor countries who now want family planning. This is the equivalent of a donation of only seven dollars per person per year from each citizen in the developed countries.[132] How many people would donate the price of a movie each year to significantly reduce the growth of human populations in developing countries?

Conclusion

As we look into the future, we find that a majority of the earth's people face enormous problems. As much as we may wish to turn our back on these issues, we cannot. Their problems are also ours. If not for moral or ethical reasons, we must enable them to build a decent life for themselves in their country in order to preserve our own quality of life. If the poor majority are given an opportunity to gain political and economic control of their own destinies, they will rebuild their societies and fully participate in a new and prosperous world. If they are not allowed to meet their basic needs in their own country, they will come to ours in massive and unsustainable numbers.

CHAPTER ELEVEN

NATIONAL DEFENSE AND WORLD SECURITY

History

Nuclear warfare began when two relativity small atomic bombs were exploded over the cities of Hiroshima and Nagasaki in 1945. The casualties included approximately 240,000 initial deaths and thousands more who later died of radiation sickness, leukemia and other forms of cancer.[133] For the next forty-five years, the massive nuclear arsenals of both the U.S. and the Soviet Union prevented World War III. The stabilizing deterrence was the belief by both adversaries that their opponent's weapons could be used and that the results would be mutual terror and destruction. During this nuclear standoff, the superpowers continued to export conventional weapons to the poor developing countries. Their "foreign aid" was used primarily to support small scale wars fought by their surrogates.

Then a bankrupt Soviet Union, faced with a revolt first by its satellite nations and then its republics, threw off communism for democracy and disintegrated as a nation. The world stood in stunned and unbelieving silence as the cold war ended; almost without a shot fired. As a result, with the exception of the oil rich Middle East, many developing countries lost their strategic importance and thus their supply of American or Soviet weapons.

Current Wars

As the demand for democracy swept the world, many of these struggling nations attempted to establish representative governments through either revolution or negotiation. For those who were successful, the illusion of immediate peace and economic prosperity was short lived. The lengthy list of basic problems still existed: territorial disputes, religious conflicts, scarce resources, lack of education, poverty, overpopulation, racism, tribalism, corruption and political and economic exploitation by a wealthy elite. Smoldering historical hatreds, no longer suppressed by the superpowers, were fanned by political, social and economic instability and the resulting conflicts were fueled by the lucrative world arms trade. The wars in these poor countries were and still are long, low intensity conflicts fought primarily with poor quality forces and weapons. Typically they do not result in victory and a resolution of the disagreements but end in a stalemate of exhaustion. Failing to resolve the issues, they often set the stage for the next conflict.[58] They do continue to produce the predictable and disastrous fruits of war. Masses of women, children and elderly flee the destruction of their homes and communities with a few meager belongings to a life of squalor, disease and starvation in refugee camps.

Weapons

In an attempt to maintain power, many of these national leaders divert their country's income to the purchase of weapons. The developing countries with vital natural resources, such as the oil rich middle eastern nations, are able to purchase expensive and sophisticated armaments from such diverse sources as the United States, China, North Korea and the giant war surplus sale in Eastern Europe and the former Soviet Union. For the right price the market will even provide the materials and technology needed to produce chemical, biological and nuclear weapons. It is estimated that by the year 2000, sixty countries (one out of every three) will either have nuclear weapons or the capability to build and disperse them.[133] At the same time the number of "poor man's atomic bombs", chemical and biological weapons, will continue to proliferate. Approximately twenty countries are developing chemical weapons which are both inexpensive and easily produced and at least ten countries are believed to have biological warfare capabilities.[36] With the purchase or construction of more and larger missiles, they will increase their ability to distribute these deadly devices.

Potential Future Wars

As we look into the near future, there are at least two areas of the world where nuclear war could be imminent. The following theoretical future scenarios describe how this disastrous event could unfold. In the Middle East, despite recent successful negotiations between Israel and the PLO, the quality of life will continue to deteriorate for most of the people in the poor, non oil producing countries due to historical hostilities, increasing populations and a decline in basic necessities, primarily water.[132] Many will respond to their desperate situation by turning inward to Moslem fundamentalism. A series of major terrorist incidents carried out by militant fundamentalists against western nations and Israel could bring the promised "surgical" military response by the Israeli military. This would, in turn, result in a demand for a holy war against the hated Israelis and their American supporters. In order to prevent the loss of political control and possible civil war within their own deteriorating countries, many Middle Eastern political leaders would acquiesce to these demands. Surrounded by a somewhat unified and fanatical force which possessed chemical and nuclear weapons, the Israeli militant right could be swept into power. A reluctance on the part of the American people to continue to support expensive and indecisive Middle Eastern wars would leave Israel in a desperate situation. In an attempt to insure the survival of their country, the military could unleash a massive nuclear first strike on strategic targets in the surrounding countries. If these events occurred, the enraged people of the Moslem nations could be unified in a war against Israel.[57]

The second area of the world which presses on the hair trigger of nuclear war is the subcontinental region of India and Pakistan. The persistent and currently increasing conflict is of grave concern to those who study this area. Within India, there has been chronic discontent between Hindus, who make up a majority of the population, and Moslems. Battles over holy places have raged between fundamentalists of both religions and over-population and poverty continues to fuel these conflicts. In the future, the resulting disunity could destroy the democratic government. This situation would be aggravated by the volatile bordering country of Kashmir where Hindu fundamentalists periodically battle Moslem guerrillas. The conflict in Kashmir and also the border clashes between India and

Pakistan could eventually develop into a full scale war. Both countries have nuclear weapons and if one combatant suffers heavy losses of troops or territory, the war could escalate into a nuclear conflict.

The American Role

How should the only remaining superpower respond to these growing threats to world peace? We have several options. Since we have established trading relationships with, and military superiority over other developed countries, we could assume an isolationist position and let the poor countries of the world fend for themselves. As tempting as this may appear, abdicating our strong economic and military position in these areas of the world would invite a host of potential aggressors to initiate local wars or increase terrorist activities in international air transportation or within the United States. We would ultimately be drawn into the small wars in foreign countries in order to protect our access to critical imports such as petroleum and in an attempt to defend ourselves against terrorism.

Another possible strategy is to expend a major portion of our resources on defense, remain the single dominant military power and function as the world police officer. But this will eventually lead to our financial decline. The wealthy Asian and European countries, while hiding under America's military skirts, can surpass us economically by continuing to invest in technological development and the production of consumer goods.

United Nations

There is another option for America and the other countries of the world that seek to eliminate war as a method of resolving human conflict. Using a strengthened United Nations as a unifying organization, we could develop a strategy for world peace that is based upon several concepts.

The first is a national defense force in each country which is designed around "minimum necessary deterrence". Through international negotiation, the type and number of weapons could be limited to those needed to inflict unacceptable damage upon a potentially aggressive enemy. The resulting military stability would be followed by continuing arms control and reduction agreements. This could include a decrease in the development and sale of new, expensive, high technology weapons systems. This is a critical point because the development of these weapons is often self-perpetuating. For example, after American taxpayers spend billions of dollars on research, development and the construction of new weapons, many are sold to our allies who can resell or give them to other countries. Eventually many fall into the hands of our current or potential enemies. We must then spend more money to develop new, more effective weapons which are capable of destroying those which we previously designed.

Through international cooperation we can succeed in finding peace in a middle ground between a secure national defense for each individual country and a strong United Nations whose members will cede enough economic support and political and military power to enable it to function effectively. The increasing number of unstable countries in the world with both modern, conventional arms and weapons of mass destruction require that we develop strong collective world security. The recent war between United Nations forces and Iraq is a case in point. The extent to which the conflict was successful continues to be debated. However, after a long period of preparation, a UN force was mobilized. It consisted primarily of U.S. military with minor support from our historical allies and rental troops from countries such as Turkey and Syria. The Iraqi army was successfully driven from Kuwait and the peace accords that followed attempted to prevent Iraq from waging future wars. However, despite this major effort, many problems still exist. The regime that started the war is still in control of Iraq and Jordan continues to violate the embargo.

Prevention of War

It is easier and less expensive to prevent a war than to fight one. A strengthened United Nations could prevent many wars with an active program of peace building. This includes the reduction of poverty, injustice and other factors that eventually lead to war. U.N. peace building groups must be enlarged and improved. Their membership should include heads of state, international courts and professional arbitrators. They should be in session constantly as they attempt to mediate all major national and international disputes, This includes tribal, racial, ethnic, religious and political conflicts within nations and also disputes between different countries regarding territories, borders and resource rights. This appears to be an impossible task however in order to be effective, all members need not agree on the final proposals. They must only reach consensus. If most agree and others are neutral, then resolution can occur. Also proposed solutions are more successful if those in conflict have accurate and well-distributed information regarding themselves and their opponents. Public opinion can then be used to move toward a peaceful resolution.

Since most U.N. member nations will benefit from peace rather than war, other countries could offer positive inducements to those negotiating to resolve their conflicts. These would include economic aid, improved trade relations or loan forgiveness. If adversaries fail to negotiate in good faith or violate established agreements, a majority of the U.N. member nations would respond with massive and sustained economic pressure against the offending groups or countries. Possible examples include loss of foreign aid, sanctions, travel and trade restrictions, product boycotts and a ban on participation in international events. More severe measures could include freezing funds in foreign banks and embargoes or blockades on items other than food and medical supplies. When possible, pressure should be exerted on the leaders who make the decisions rather than the people who suffer from the consequences of these determinations. Few isolated nations can survive and most would resolve their conflicts.[58]

If War Comes

If these techniques of negotiated resolution fail and armed conflict occurs, the next phase could be initiated. A highly trained, standing international peacekeeping force would quickly be dispatched in an attempt to separate the combatants, establish a cease fire, develop neutral zones between opposing forces and move warring groups into negotiations. Peace-keeping forces have been most successful if selection is based upon their historical, cultural and social relationship to those groups in conflict and if combatants want to end the fighting but are not able to do so.

If the peacekeeping force is unable to stop the fighting and an offensive military response is judged to be appropriate and necessary, the next phase could be initiated. A fully offensive, international military strike force would be quickly mobilized and dispatched. In response to civil wars or border conflicts, this force could separate or isolate combatants while negotiations are initiated. If one country attacks another, invading forces could be driven out of the nation and their offensive weapons destroyed.

Future Peace?

At this point we still have a choice. Through international agreements we can move toward peace in many ways. These include establishing a secure national defense for all countries, reducing conventional armaments and eliminating the uncontrollable weapons of mass destruction through a phased and verifiable international program of aerial surveillance and the computer tracking of international business transactions involving the purchase or production of weapons.

As a group of humans who share the same planet, we must adopt the wisdom of those who abolished dueling. The purpose of the duel was to identify a winner; however, when pistols replaced swords, both participants were often killed. With no victor, the duel had no purpose and as a result the practice ceases.[133] War as a means of resolving conflicts can no longer be supported politically or economically in the new global village.

CHAPTER TWELVE

CONCLUSION

W e are led by politicians who do not represent the best interests of our nation. They are controlled primarily by special interest groups which finance political campaigns in exchange for favorable legislation. As a result, a majority of the American people now struggle under massive economic, social and environmental debt. Grassroots groups attempt to influence politicians however they lack sufficient power, and have met with limited success.

An alternative to our current situation is a "reformed" Ross Perot and a new group of skilled and creative congressional candidates. Without obligations to special interests, they can develop a political platform with realistic and workable solutions. These proposals will be supported by citizens who are united by a fear of future insecurity. The ideas will be activated by economic incentives and disincentives and a revival of our ethics, patriotism and religious faiths.

The tools used to carry out this task will be education and technology. In the process of national restoration we will confront our cultural practices and traditions, preserving those which provide a needed connection to our rich past and discarding those which block our route to a successful future. We will be guided primarily by two concepts, sustainability and efficiency. Within a closed and finite biosphere, we will reduce birth rates, consumption and waste production. Simultaneously we can establish a society with good jobs, functional families and communities and mutual respect. A major reduction in government and private sector waste and corruption will result in increased efficiency and productivity.

We must also maintain our leadership in the new world village. As multinational business penetrates world markets, we must motivate governments to insure economic and social justice for their people. Poor nations will be assisted with small scale development which will enable the people to improve their own quality of life. Member countries will provide the United Nations with sufficient power and resources needed to maintain peace or stop wars.

The reinventing of America will be exciting, creative and at times even chaotic. Although we will be continually buffeted by major forces which are already rapidly converging upon us, carefully developed plans and programs, supported by the vision of a new and better future, will enable us to prevail.

BIBLIOGRAPHY

1. Aaron, Henry T. and William B. Swartz. The Painful Prescription: Rationing Health Care. Washington D.C.: The Brookings Institute, 1984.

2. Adler, Freda, Gerhard O. W. Mueller and William Laufer. Criminology. New York: McGraw-Hill, Inc., 1991.

3. Angel, David, Jr., Justin Comer and Matthew L. N. Wilkinson (eds.). Sustaining the Earth: Response to Environmental Threats. New York: St. Martin Press, 1990.

4. Asimov, Isaac and Fredrick Pohl. Our Angry Earth. New York: Tom Doherty Associates, 1991.

5. Aspen Institute. The Americas in a New World: The 1990 Report of the Inter-American Dialogue. Queenstown, Maryland: Aspen Institute Publications Office, 1990, pp. 1-88.

6. Austin, Richard. Reclaiming America: Restoring Nature to Culture. Abingdon, VA: Creekside Press, 1990.

7. Barkley, Paul W. and David W. Seckler. Environmental Growth and Economic Decay: The Solution Becomes the Problem. San Diego: Harcourt Brace, Jovanovich, 1972.

8. Barnes, Fred, "Loving Too Much," <u>New Republic</u>, No. 6, August 1993, pp. 10-12

9. Barrett, Laurence, "A Marriage of Convenience," <u>Time</u>, No. 1, July 1993, pp. 36-38

10. Barzelay, Michael. <u>Breaking Through Bureaucracy: A New Vision for Managing in Government</u>. Berkeley, CA: University of California Press, 1992.

11. Batra, Ravi. <u>The Great Depression of 1990</u>. New York: Simon and Schuster, 1988.

12. Berry, Thomas. <u>The Dream of the Earth</u>. San Francisco: Sierra Club Books, 1990.

13. Berry, Wendell. <u>The Unsettling of America: Culture and Agriculture</u>. San Francisco: Sierra Club Books, 1986.

14. Berry, Wendell. <u>The Gift of Good Land</u>. Berkeley, California: North Point Press, 1981.

15. Berry, Wendell. <u>Home Economics</u>. San Francisco: North Point Press, 1987.

16. Bloom, Allan. <u>The Closing of the American Mind</u>. New York: Simon and Schuster, 1987.

17. Bodansky, Yassef. <u>Target America: Terrorism in the U.S. Today</u>. New York: Shapolski Publishers, 1993.

18. Borger, Gloria and Jerry Buckley, "Perot Keeps Going and Going," <u>U.S. News and World Report</u>, No. 19, May 1993, pp. 36-43

19. Boswell, Terry (ed.). <u>Revolution in the World System</u>. Westport, Connecticut: Greenwood Press, 1989.

20. Boulding, Kenneth E. <u>Three Faces of Power</u>. Troy, New York: Sage Publications, 1989.

21. Bouza, Anthony. <u>How to Stop Crime</u>. New York: Plenum Press, 1993.

22. Bowles, Samuel, David M. Gordon, et al. <u>After the Wasteland: A Democratic Economics for the Year 2000</u>. New York: M. E. Simple, Inc., 1990.

23. Boyer, William H. <u>America's Future: Transition to the 21st Century</u>. New York: Prager, 1984.

24. Brecher, Edward M.. <u>Licit and Illicit Drugs: The Consumers Union Report on Narcotics, Stimulants, Depressants, Inhalants, Hallucinogens and Marijuana—Including Caffeine, Nicotine and Alcohol</u>. New York: Consumers Union, 1972.

25. Brockway, George C.. <u>The End of Economic Man</u>. New York: Norton, 1993.

26. Brogan, Patrick. <u>The Fighting Never Stopped</u>. New York: Random House, 1990.

27. Brown, Lester R. <u>Building a Sustainable Society</u>. New York: W. W. Norton, 1981.

28. Brown, Lester R., "The New World Order," in Lester R. Brown, et al (eds.), <u>State of the World: 1991</u>. New York: W. W. Norton & Company, 1991.

29. Calleo, David. <u>The Bankrupting of America: How the Federal Budget is Impoverishing the Nation</u>. New York: William Morrow and Companies, 1992.

30. Carey, Art. The United States of Incompetence. Boston, MA: Houghton Mifflin, 1991.

31. Carlson, Richard and Bruce Goldman. 2020 Visions: Long View of a Changing World. Stanford, California: Stanford Alumni Association, 1990.

32. Casti, John L.. Searching for Certainty: What Scientists Can Know About the Future. New York: William Morrow and Company, 1990.

33. Castro, Janice, "Condition Critical," Time Magazine, No. 21, November 25, 1991, pp. 34-42

34. Cetron, Marvin and Margaret Gayle. Educational Renaissance: Our Schools at the Turn of the Century. New York: St. Martins Press, 1991.

35. Cetron, Marvin and Owen Davies. American Renaissance: Our Life at the Turn of the 21st Century. New York: St. Martin's Press, 1989.

36. Cetron, Marvin and Owen Davis. Crystal Globe: The Haves and the Have Nots of the New World Order. New York: St. Martin Press, 1991.

37. Chancellor, John. Peril and Promise: A Commentary on America. New York: Harper and Row, 1990.

38. Clark, W. C. and R. E. Munn (eds.). Sustainable Development of the Biosphere. Cambridge, Massachusetts: Cambridge University Press, 1986.

39. Clawson, Dan, Alan Neustadtl, et al. Money Talks: Corporate PACS and Political Influence. New York: Basic Books, 1992.

40. Cleveland, Harlan, "Rethinking International Governance: Coalition Politics in an Unruly World," The Futurist, No. 3, May-June 1991, pp. 20-27

41. Cloud, Stanley W. and Richard Woodbury, "The Lessons of Perot," Time Magazine, No. 20, November 1992, pp. 69-71

42. Coates, Gary J. (ed.). Resettling America: Energy, Ecology and Community. Hanover, Massachusetts: Brick House, 1981.

43. Collard, David and David Pearce, et al (ed.). Economics, Growth and Sustainable Environments. New York: St. Martin Press, 1988.

44. Committee on the Role of Alternative Farming Methods in Modern Production Agriculture, Board of Agriculture National Research Council. Alternative Agriculture. Washington, D.C.: National Academy Press, 1989.

45. Cornish, Edward (ed.). 1999: The World of Tomorrow. Washington, D.C.: World Future Society, 1978.

46. Cornish, Edward. Global Solutions: Innovative Approaches to World Problems. Washington, D.C.: World Future Society, 1984.

47. Crosson, Pierre R. and Norman Rosenberg. "Strategies for Agriculture." Scientific American, Vol. 261, No. 3, September 1989, pp. 128-136.

48. Currie, Elliott. Reckoning: Drugs, the Cities and the American Future. New York: Hill and Wang, 1993.

49. Cutterbuck, Richard. Terrorism and Guerrilla Warfare. New York: Routledge, Chapman and Hall, 1990.

50. Daly, Herman, John Cobb. For the Common Good: Redirecting the Economy Toward Community, the Environment and a Sustainable Future. Boston: Beacon Press, 1989.

51. Daly, Herman E. (ed.). Economics, Ecology, Ethics: Essays Toward a Steady State Economy. New York: Freeman, 1980.

52. DeSoto, Hernando. The Other Path: The Invisible Revolution in the Third World. New York: Harper and Row, 1989.

53. Dionne Jr., E. J.. Why Americans Hate Politics. New York: Simon and Schuster, 1991.

54. Dobb, Edwin, "Plan for a Small Planet," Audubon, No. 3, May-June 1992, pp. 94-97

55. Drucker, Peter F.. Post Capitalist Society. New York: Harper, 1993.

56. Drucker, Peter F.. The New Realities: In Government and Politics: In Economics and Business: In Society and World Views. New York: Harper and Row, 1989.

57. Dunningan, James F. and Austin Bay. A Quick and Dirty Guide to War: Briefings on Present and Potential Wars. New York: William Morrow and Company, 1991.

58. Dunningan, James F. and William Martel. How to Stop a War: The Lessons of Two Hundred Years of War and Peace. New York: Doubleday, 1987.

59. Durning, Alan, "Limiting Consumption: Toward a Sustainable Culture," The Futurist, No. 4, July-August 1991, pp. 11-15

60. Durning, Alan D. "Asking How Much is Enough," in Lester R. Brown et al (eds.), State of the World: 1991. New York: W. W. Norton, 1991, pp.153-170.

61. Ehrenhalt, Alan. <u>The United States of Ambition: Politics, Power and the Pursuit of Office</u>. New York: Times Books, 1992.

62. Ehrlich, Anne H. and John W. Birks (ed.). <u>Hidden Dangers, Environmental Consequences fo Preparing for War</u>. San Francisco: Sierra Club Books, 1990.

63. Ehrlich, Paul and Anne Ehrlich. <u>The Population Explosion</u>. New York: Simon and Schuster, 1990.

64. Ehrlich, Paul R., John P. Holden (eds.). <u>The Cassandra Conference: Resources and the Human Predicament</u>. College Station, Texas: Texas A & M University Press, 1988.

65. Etzioni, Amitai. <u>The Moral Dimension: Toward a New Economics</u>. New York: Macmillan, 1988.

66. Feather, Frank. <u>G Forces: The 35 Global Forces Restructuring Our Future</u>. New York: William Morrow and Co., Inc., 1989.

67. Feldstein, Martin, Ed.. <u>The Risk of Economic Crisis</u>. Chicago, IL: University of Chicago Press, 1991.

68. Ferrarotti, Franco. <u>Five Scenarios for the Year 2000</u>. Westport Connecticut: Greenwood Press, 1986.

69. Fineman, Howard, "Ross Perot's New Army," <u>Newsweek</u>, No. 23, June 1993, pp. 24-26

70. Flexner, Kurt F. <u>The Enlightened Society: The Economy with a Human Face</u>. Lexington, Massachusetts: D. C. Heath, 1989.

71. Flynn, John C. <u>Cocaine: An In Depth Look at the Facts, Science, History and Future of the World's Most Addictive Drug</u>. New York: Carol Publishing Group, 1991.

72. Fotion, Neal and G. Elfstrom. Military Ethics: Guidelines for Peace and War. Boston, MA: Routledge and Kegan Paul Press, 1986.

73. Freudenberger, C. Dean. Global Dust Bowl: Can We Stop the Destruction of the Land Before it is Too Late? Minneapolis: Augsberg Fortress, 1990.

74. Friedman, Benjamin M.. Day of Reckoning: The Consequences of American Economic Policy. New York: Random House, 1989.

75. Gever, John, Robert Kaufmann, et al. Beyond Oil: The Threat to Food and Fuel in the Coming Decades. Cambridge, Massachusetts: Bellinger Publishing Company, 1986.

76. Gibbons, John H. et al. "Strategies for Energy Use." Scientific American. September 1989, Vol. 261, No. 3, pp. 136-143.

77. Goodman, David, Michael Redclift (eds.), The International Farm Crisis. New York: St. Martin, 1989.

78. Goodwin, Richard. Promises to Keep: A Call for a New American Revolution. New York: Times Books, 1992.

79. Gordon, Anita and David Suzuki. It's a Matter of Survival. Cambridge, Massachusetts: Harvard University Press, 1991.

80. Greider, William. Who Will Tell The People: Betrayal of American Democracy. New York: Simon and Schuster, 1992.

81. Gross, Martin L. The Government Racket: Washington Waste from A to Z. New York: Bantam Books, 1992.

82. Gwertzman, Bernard and Michael T. Kaufman, (eds.). The Collapse of Communism. New York: Random House, 1990.

83. Haas, Lawrence. <u>Running on Empty: Bush Congress and the Politics of a Bankrupt Government</u>. Homewood, IL: Business One Irwin, 1990.

84. Halberstam, David. <u>The Next Century</u>. New York: William Morrow Co., Inc., 1991.

85. Handy, Charles. <u>THe Age of Unreason</u>. Boston: Harvard Business School Press, 1989.

86. Harris, Jonathan. <u>World Agriculture and the Environment</u>. New York: Garland Publishing, Inc., 1990.

87. Harrison, Lawrence E.. <u>Who Prospers: How Cultural Values Shape Economic and Political Success</u>. New York: Basic Books, 1992.

88. Hayden Delores. <u>Redesigning the American Dream: The Future of Housing, Work and Family Life</u>. New York: W. W. Norton & Company, 1984.

89. Heilbroner, Robert and Peter Bernstein. <u>The Debt and the Deficit: False Alarms, Real Possibilities</u>. New York: W. W. Norton Co., 1989.

90. Hewlett, Sylvia Ann. <u>When the Bough Breaks: The Cost of Neglecting our Children</u>. New York: Houghton Mifflin, 1991.

91. Hightower, Jame E. (ed.). <u>Caring for Folks From Birth to Death</u>. Nashville, Tennessee: Broadman Press, 1985.

92. Hollins, Harry B. et al. <u>The Conquest of War: Alternative Strategies for Global Security</u>. Boulder, Colorado: Westview Press, 1989.

93. Holloway, Marguerite and Paul Wallich, "A Risk Worth Taking," <u>Scientific American</u>, No. 5, November 1992, p. 126

94. Hunter, Kenneth W. "Big Messes," The Futurist. January-February, 1991, Vol. 25, No. 1, pp. 10-17.

95. Jackson, Larry, "Keeping the Faith: Western Religion's Future," The Futurist, No. 5, October 1985, p. 26-27

96. Jackson, Wes et al (eds). Meeting the Expectations of the Land: Essays in Sustainable Agriculture and Stewardship. Berkeley: North Point Press, 1984.

97. Jackson, Wes. Alter of Unhewn Stone: Science and the Earth. San Francisco: North Point Press, 1987.

98. Jackson, Wes. New Roots for Agriculture. San Francisco: Friends of the Earth, 1980.

99. Jay, Peter, Michael Stewart. Apocalypse 2000. London: Sidgwick and Jackson, 1987.

100. Johnson, D. Gale and John A. Schnittkler. U.S. Agriculture in a World Context: Policies and Approaches for the Next Decade. New York: Praeger Publishers, 1974.

101. Johnston, William B., Kevin R. Hopkins. The Catastrophe Ahead: AIDS and the Case for a New Public Policy. New York: Prager, 1990.

102. Kahn, Herman. World Economic Development: 1979 and Beyond. Boulder, Colorado: Westview Press, 1979.

103. Kearns, David T. and Denis Doyle. Winning the Brain Race: A Bold Plan to Make Our Schools Competitive. San Francisco: Institute for Contemporary Studies, 1988.

104. Keegan, John and Andrew Wheatcroft. Zones of Conflict: An Atlas of Future Wars. New York: Simon and Shuster, 1986.

105. Kennedy, Paul. Preparing for the Twenty-First Century. New York: Random House, 1993.

106. Kennedy, Paul. The Rise and Fall of the Great Powers: Economic Change and Military Conflict from 1500 to 2000. New York: Random House, 1987.

107. Keyfitz, Nathan. "The Growing Human Population." Scientific American. September 1989, Vol. 261, No. 3, pp. 118-127.

108. Kidder, Rushworth, M. An Agenda for the 21st Century. Boston: Christian Science Publishing Society, 1987.

109. Kilko, Joyce. Restructuring the World Economy. New York: Pantheon Books, 1988.

110. Korten, David C. Getting to the 21st Century. West Hartford, Connecticut, 1990.

111. Kutzner, Patricia L.. Contemporary World Issues: World Hunger A Reference Handbook. Santa Barbara, CA: ABC-CL 10 Inc., 1991.

112. Lamm, Richard. Hard Choices. Denver: State of Colorado, 1985.

113. Lapp, Frances Moore et al. Food First: Beyond the Myth of Scarcity. Boston: Houghton Mifflin, 1977.

114. Lawrence, Robert A. and Charles L. Schultze (ed.). An American Trade Strategy Options for the 1990's. Washington D.C.: The Brookings Institute, 1990.

115. Lewis, Anne. Restructuring America's Schools. Arlington, Virginia: American Association of School Administrators, 1989.

116. Lewis, H. W.. Technological Risk. New York: W. W. Norton Co., 1990.

117. Lewis, Hunter and Donald Allison. The Real World War: The Coming Battle for the New Global Economy and Why We Are in Danger of Losing It.. New York: Coward, McCann and Geoghegan, 1982.

118. Lienberger, Paul and Bruce Tucker. The New Individualists: The Generation After the Organization Man. New York: Harper Collins Publishers, 1991.

119. Lifton, Robert J. and Richard Falk. Indefensible Weapons: The Political and Psychological Case Against Nuclearism. New York: Basic Books, 1982.

120. Lovins, Amory B. World Energy Strategies: Facts, Issues and Options. San Francisco: Friends of the Earth International, 1975.

121. Lovins, Amory B., L. Hunter Lovins. Brittle Power: Energy Strategy for National Security. Anover, Massachusetts: Brick House, 1982.

122. Lovins, Hunter L. et al. Energy Unbound: A Fable for American Future. San Francisco: Sierra Book Club, 1986.

123. Lowenthal, Abraham F.. Partners in Conflict: The United States and Latin America in the 1990's. Baltimore, Maryland: John Hopkins University Press, 1990.

124. MacNeill, Jim. "Strategies for Sustainable Economic Development." Scientific American. September 1989, Vol. 261, No. 3, pp. 154-165.

125. Malabre Jr., Alfred. Beyond Our Means: How Reckless Borrowing Now Threatens to Overwhelm Us. New York: Random House, 1988.

126. Malabre, Jr., Alfred. <u>Understanding the New Economy</u>. Homewood, Illinois: Dow Jones-Irwin, 1989.

127. Mauer, Mark. <u>Report on Americans Behind Bars</u>. Washington, D.C.: The Sentencing Project, 1991, pp. 1-20.

128. Mc Cullough, David and David Grubin. <u>Smithsonian World: Farming</u>. WETA-TV: Smithsonian Institute and WETA-TV, 1987.

129. McCord, William. <u>Voyages to Utopia: From Monastery to Commune: The Search for the Perfect Society in Modern Times</u>. New York: W. W. Norton Co., 1989.

130. Meir, Alan et al. <u>Supplying Energy Through Greater Efficiency: The Potential for Conservation in California's Residential Sector</u>. Berkeley: University of California Press, 1983.

131. Miller, Alan S. <u>Gaia Connection: An Introduction to Ecology, Ecoethics and Economies</u>. Lanham, Maryland: Rowman and Littlefield, 1991.

132. Miller, G. Tyler. <u>Environmental Science: Sustaining the Earth</u>. Belmont, California: Wadsworth, 1990.

133. Miller, G. Tyler. <u>Living in the Environment: An Introduction to Environmental Science</u>. Belmont, California: Wadsworth, 1991.

134. Morris, Charles R.. <u>The Coming Global Boom: How to Benefit Now From Tomorrows Dynamic World Economy</u>. New York: Bantam Books, 1990.

135. Murray, Charles. <u>Losing Ground: American Social Policy 1950-1980</u>. New York: Basic Books, 1984.

136. Nagel, Stuart S.. <u>Higher Goals for America: Doing Better Than the Best</u>. New York: University Press of America, 1989.

137. Naisbitt, John and Patricia Aburdene. <u>Megatrends 2000: Ten New Directions for the 1990s</u>. New York: William Morrow and Co., 1990.

138. Nau, Henry R. <u>The Myth of America's Decline: Leading the World Into The 1990s</u>. New York: Oxford University Press, 1990.

139. Nelson, Robert H. <u>Reaching for Heaven on Earth: The Theological Meaning of Economics</u>. Savage, Maryland: Rowman and Littlefield Publishers, Inc., 1991.

140. Nolan, Janne, E. <u>Guardians of the Arsenal: The Politics of Nuclear Strategy</u>. New York: Basic Books, Inc., 1989.

141. Ohmae, Kenichi. <u>The Borderless World: Power and Strategy in the Interlinked Economy</u>. New York: Harper Collins, 1990.

142. Osborne, David and Ted Graebler, <u>Reinventing Government: How the Entrepreneurial Spirit is Transforming the Public Sector From Schoolhouse to Statehouse, City Hall to the Pentagon</u>. New York: Addison-Wesley, 1992.

143. Pastor, Robert A. and Jorge Castañeda. <u>Limits to Friendship: The United States and Mexico</u>. New York: Alfred A. Knopf, 1988.

144. Patterson, James and Peter Kim. <u>The Day America Told the Truth: What People Really Believe about Everything That Really Matters</u>. New York: Prentice-Hall Press, 1990.

145. Payne, James. <u>Costly Returns: The Burdens of the U.S. Tax System</u>. San Francisco: Institute of Contemporary Studies, 1993.

146. Peck, Jonathan, "Optimistic Outlook for U.S. Health," <u>The Futurist</u>, No. 4, July-August 1991, p. 41

147. Perot, Ross. <u>United We Stand: How We Can Take Back Our Country</u>. New York: Hyperion, 1992.

148. Peters, Charles. <u>How Washington Really Works</u>. Reading, MA: Addison Wesley, 1992.

149. Peters, Thomas J. and Robert Waterman, Jr. <u>In Search of Excellence</u>. New York: Harper and Row, 1982.

150. Peterson, Peter G. and Neil Howe. <u>On Borrowed Time: How the Growth in Entitlement Spending Threatens America</u>. San Francisco: Future Institute for Contemporary Studies, 1988.

151. Pollock, Cynthia, "Decommissioning: Nuclear Powers Missing Link," <u>Worldwatch Paper</u>, No. 69, April 1986, 1-23

152. Postel, Sandra and Christopher Flaven. "Reshaping the Global Economy," in Lester R. Brown et al (eds.), <u>State of the World: 1991</u>. New York: W. W. Norton and Company, 1991.

153. Reich, Charles A.. <u>The Greening of America: How the Youth Revolution is Trying to Make America Livable</u>. New York: Random House, 1970.

154. Reich, Robert R. <u>The Work of Nations: Preparing Ourselves for 21st Century Capitalism</u>. New York: Alfred A. Knopf, 1991.

155. Reich, Robert B.. <u>The Next American Frontier</u>. New York: Times Books, 1983.

156. Renner, Michael. <u>National Security: The Economic and Environmental Dimensions</u>. Washington, D.C.: World Watch Institute, 1989.

157. Repetto, Robert (ed.). <u>The Global Possible: Resources, Development and the New Century</u>. New Haven, Connecticut: Yale University Press, 1985.

158. Rifkin, Jeremy. <u>Biosphere Politics: A New Conciousness for a New Century</u>. New York: Crown Publishers, 1991.

159. Robbins, John. <u>Diet For A New America</u>. Walpole, New Hampshire: Stillpoint Publishing, 1987.

160. Robertson, James. <u>Future Wealth: A New Economics for the 21st Century</u>. London: Cassell Publishers, 1990.

161. Rock, James M. (ed.). <u>Debt and the Twin Deficits Debate</u>. Mountain View, California: Mayfield Publishing Company, 1991.

162. Ross, Perot. <u>Not For Sale at Any Price: How We Can Save America For Our Children</u>. New York: Hyperion, 1993.

163. Ruckelshaus, William D. "Toward a Sustainable World." <u>Scientific American</u>. September 1989, Vol. 261, No. 3, pp. 166-175.

164. Saaty, Thomas L. and Larry W. Boone. <u>Embracing the Future</u>. New York: Praeger, 1990.

165. Sadik, Nafis. "World Population Continues to Rise." <u>The Futurist</u>. March-April 1991, Vol. 25, No. 2, pp. 9-14.

166. Sagoff, Mark. <u>The Economy of the Earth: Philosophy, Law and the Environment</u>. New York: Cambridge University Press, 1988.

167. Satin, Mark. <u>New Options for America: The Second American Experiment has Begun</u>. Fresno, CA: The Press at California State University, Fresno, 1991.

168. Schmookler, Andrew, "The Insatiable Society: Materialistic Values and Human Needs," <u>The Futurist</u>, No. 4, July-August 1991, pp. 17-19

169. Schneider, Bertrand. The Barefoot Revolution: A Report to the Club of Rome. London: IT Publications, 1988.

170. Schoultze, Lars. National Security and United States Policy Toward Latin America. Princeton, New Jersey: Princeton University, 1987.

171. Shames, Lawrence. The Hunger for More: Searching for Values in an Age of Greed. New York: Random House, 1989.

172. Siberman, Charles E.. Criminal Violence: Criminal Justice. New York: Random House, 1978.

173. Silk, Leonard. Economics in Plain English. New York: Simon and Schuster, 1986.

174. Simmons, J. L.. Future Lives: A Fearless Guide to Our Transitional Times. Santa Fe, New Mexico: Bear and Company, 1990.

175. Simon, Julian L., Herman Kahn. The Resourceful Earth: A Response to Global 2000. New York: Basil Blackwell, 1984.

176. Smith, G. D.. Combating Terrorism. New York: Routledge, 1990.

177. Solkoff, Joel. The Politics of Food: The Decline of Agriculture and the Rise of Agribusiness in America. San Francisco: Sierra Club Books, 1985.

178. Sorauf, Frank J. and Paul Beck. Party Politics in America. 6th ed., Boston, Massachusetts: Scott Foresman and Company, 1988.

179. Starke, Linda. Signs of Hope: Working Toward Our Common Future. New York: Oxford University Press, 1990.

180. Staten, Jay. The Embattled Farms. Golden, Colorado: Fulcrum, Inc., 1987.

181. Strange, Marty. Family Farming: A New Economic Vision. Lincoln, Nebraska: University of Nebraska Press, 1989.

182. Strasser, Susan. Satisfaction Guaranteed: The Making of American Mass Marketing. New York: Random House, 1989.

183. Thurow, Lester C. The Zero Sum Solution: Building a World Class American Economy. New York: Simon and Schuster, 1985.

184. Turner, Kerry R. (ed.). Sustainable Environmental Management: Principles and Practice. Boulder, Colorado: Westview Press, 1988.

185. Ulrich, Hugh. Losing Ground: Agricultural Policy and the Decline of the American Farm. Chicago, Illinois: Chicago Review Press, 1989.

186. United Nations. Global Outlook 2000: An Economic Social and Environmental Perspective. New York: United Nations Publications, 1990.

187. Wachtel, Paul. The Poverty of Affluence. Philadelphia: New Society Publishers, 1989.

188. Wager, Warren W. A Short History of the Future. Chicago: University of Chicago Press, 1989.

189. White, Theodore H. America in Search of Itself: The Making of the President: 1956-1980. New York: Harper and Row, 1982.

190. Wilentz, Sean, "Pox populi," New Republic, No. 6, August 1993, pp. 29-35

191. Willard, Timothy and Daniel Fields, "The Community in an Age of Individualism: An Interview with Amitai Etzioni," The Futurist, No. 3, May-June 1991, pp. 35-39

192. Wilson, James Q. Thinking About Crime. New York: Random House, 1985.

193. Wilson, Kenneth D. (ed.). Prospects for Growth: Changing Expectations for the Future. New York: Prager, 1977.

194. Wilson, William Julius. The Truly Disadvantaged: The Inner City, The Underclass and Public Policy. Chicago: University of Chicago, 1987.

195. World Commission on Environment and Development. Our Common Future. Oxford, England: Oxford University Press, 1987.

196. Wright, Robin and Doyle McManus. Flashpoints: Promise and Peril in a New World. New York: Alfred Knoph, 1991.

197. Yankelovich, Daniel. Coming to Public Judgement: Making Democracy Work in a Complete World. Syracuse, NY: Syracuse University Press, 1991.

198. Zinn, Howard. Declarations of Independence: Cross Examining American Ideology. New York: Harper-Collins, 1990.

ORDER FORM

NATION PUBLISHERS
10260 Hope Lane
Yucaipa, California 92399
Telephone 909 797-3068

Ordering Information

Number of Copies _____ x $~~14.95~~ 7.95 per copy = $_____.____

Sales Tax: Please add $~~1.16~~ .62 per copy for books
shipped to California addresses   _____.____

Shipping Rates: 1 book $2.00   _____.____

Additional books at $.75 each   _____.____

Air Mail (call for current price)   _____.____

Total Amount Enclosed $_____.____

Payment must be made by check or money order

Sorry, no credit cards.

Surface shipping is approximately three to four weeks.